TRANSLATOR'S NOTE

Approximately eighteen years ago, I learned from my father's relative that I am a descendent of Yaacov Yitschak Rabinovits, known as the "Yehudi HaKadosh". His granddaughter, Goldeh Layah Ruchama Rabinovits was my great grandmother and I am named after her.

In the summer of 2001, my eldest daughter and I traveled to Poland, searching for my father's roots. We visited the town of Pshis'cha, the synagogue, and the *ohel* of Rabbi Simcha Bunim and the "Yehudi HaKadosh". As my daughter, Tamar, and I stood there saying the *Kaddish* with tears in our eyes, the linkage of past and present years was immediate and direct. It was a very moving experience.

I am presently an active member of a neo-hasidic traditional synagogue affiliated with Jewish Renewal and have immersed myself in Judaic studies for several years, studying with rabbis in Vancouver and traveling to Jerusalem from time to time, to study in women's *yeshivas*. My interest in translating *Rabbi Simcha Bunim: His Life and Teachings*, by H. M. Rabinovits, occurred by happenstance. I gained the possession of this slim little volume and as I began reading it, I knew that I was meant to translate it. This has truly been a labour of love.

Rabbi Simcha Bunim lived during a time of great political instability and upheaval in Poland: the three partitions of Poland (1772, 1793, and 1795); the invasion of Napoleon's army, 1807; and the weakening of central government control. All these factors, directly and indirectly, affected the lives of Polish Jewry.

The world outlook of hasidism in central Poland as evidenced by populist hasidic leaders, *tsadikim*, such as the Seer of Lublin, Rabbi Naphtali of Ropshits, Rabbi Elimelech of Lizhensk, the Magid of Koznits and others, was characterized by a somewhat other-worldliness. It concerned itself with "signs and wonders" such as amulets, incantations and potions. They spent the bulk of their time studying, dressing uniformly in traditional hasidic garb, and creating inherited dynasties.

In contrast, chapters 1 through 8 clearly illustrate that, while Rabbi Simcha Bunim's life style (1765-1827) was that of an orthodox hasidic Jew, he was a remarkably independent minded, worldly man. Unlike the majority of the Polish-Jewish population, he spent time in Western Europe and mastered German and Italian. He continued to wear European clothing even when he was in the courts of other *tsadikim*. He earned a living as a pharmacist, which was unheard of among the *hasidim* of that time.

Populist hasidism centered on the charismatic personality of the *tsadik*, who was able to reach down to the simple, uneducated person and spiritually elevate his soul. Those *hasidim* taught that redemption could be achieved through adherence to the *tsadik*. Rabbi Simcha Bunim's emphasis on individual responsibility for the perfection of one's character traits, and his teaching of personal redemption, created a huge challenge and threat to populist hasidism. This conflict between Pshis'cha's message of personal redemption and that of populist hasidism, culminated in the famous confrontation which occurred at the wedding of a grandchild of Rabbi Avraham Yehoshua Heshel of Apta, in Ostila.

In chapters 9 through 18, the depth and purity of Rabbi Simcha Bunim's soul becomes more apparent in his essays and parables. His intelligence, wit, and devotion emerge clearly and our relationship with him deepens. We begin to feel that we know him more intimately. The hasidic tales indicate his depth of imagination and his understanding of the human dilemma. Through some of his disciples, such as Rabbi Menachem Mendel of Kotsk, Rabbi Yitschak Meir of Ger, Rabbi Hanoch of Alexander, and Rabbi Mordechai Yosef of Izbitsa, his legacy endures to this very day.

With the lack of primary sources (Rabbi Bunim never wrote down his teachings), H. M. Rabinovits relied heavily on *Kol Simcha*, written by one of his students, as well as *Ramatayim Tsofim* by Rabbi Shmuel Sheinover, Polish-Jewish history, and memories of *hasidim* tangentially connected to Rabbi Simcha Bunim. Nevertheless, he created a vivid and inspiring picture of Rabbi Simcha Bunim, his thoughts and his times.

Since I am not a hasidic scholar, I did not translate most of the footnotes, but focused rather on the content of the text. To reflect the full connotation and spirit of hasidic and traditional concepts, I retained those expressions in italicized transliteration and have provided a glossary at the end of the book. At all times I have been guided by a deep love and respect for the hasidic world of the early nineteenth century and have tried to honour its philosophy in my translation.

I would like to acknowledge and thank Rahel Halabe, a remarkable linguist who is also a well-known Israeli translator of Arabic literature. I would not have been able to accomplish this translation without her invaluable and diligent assistance. I would also like to thank my readers: Rabbi Shachar Ornstein, Dr. Leonard Angel, and Rabbi Daniel Siegel, who offered many valuable insights and suggestions. I am deeply indebted to my editor and proof reader, Hunter Taliesin, who has the eye of an eagle for detail.

Vancouver, 2007
Gloria Levi

ABOUT THE AUTHOR

Born in Uniyov, Poland, in 1908, Dr. H. M. Rabinovits came from a long line of rabbis and scribes, tracing his lineage back to the founder of the Radomsk *hasidim*, Rabbi Shlomo HaCohen, also known as "Tiferet Shlomo". He studied in the *yeshiva*, Torat Chayim, and was ordained as a rabbi in 1931.

In 1934, Dr. H. M. Rabinovits emigrated to Palestine. While working as an upholsterer in Jerusalem, he enrolled in a teachers' college and became a teacher in the predominately mystical and spiritual city of Safed, and lectured at Bar Ilan University in Tel Aviv. He later taught at Tel Aviv University, eventually becoming head of the Department of Talmud until he retired in 1977. A life-long learner, at the age of 50, Dr. Rabinovits received his doctorate from Hebrew University on *Midrashim of the Halacha and Midrashim of Agada in the Piyyutim of Yannai.*

At the age of 24, Dr. Rabinovits published his first book on the Yehudi HaKadosh, Rabbi Yaacov Yitschak of Pshis'cha. He subsequently wrote *Rabbi Simcha Bunim of Pshis'cha*, and *The Magid of Kosnets*, and received the esteemed Bialik Prize for Jewish Thought for his great book, *The Machzor of the Piyyutim of Yannai for Torah and the Holidays.*

Dr. Rabinovits also published numerous articles in various newspapers, journals, and books. A scholar who maintained a critical and objective approach to his research, his love of early hasidism in Poland, however, permeates every page of his writings, touching the soul of the reader. He died in 1991, at the age of eighty-three.

FOREWORD

Researching Polish hasidism poses certain difficulties. Researching the hasidism of Pshis'cha is even more problematic because the originators of this hasidism did not believe in writing books. Rabbi Simcha Bunim of Pshis'cha said, "I wanted to write a book called 'The Generations of Adam' that would contain the task of man and his essential nature, but I reconsidered and decided not to write it."

Neither did Rabbi Yaakov Yitschak, Ha-Yehudi of Pshis'cha, Rabbi Mendel of Kotsk, Rabbi Yitschak Meir of Gur, or Rabbi Chanoch of Alexander write books. They realized that books become holy over a period of time. Indeed, they detested everything that was fixed. They hated the fossilized, permanent forms. To them, Pshis'cha represented dynamism, vitality, and freshness. Anything that wasn't lively, that wasn't vibrant, was an abomination.

That is why, as I approached the research of Pshis'cha hasidism, my goal was to use the most reliable sources I could find. I sought to obtain data from students of Pshis'cha, from the very source of life of this sect of *hasidim*. I knew some elderly *hasidim* whose parents had personally known all the great ones of hasidism, and some who had actually known Rabbi Simcha Bunim of Pshis'cha. Comparing verbal reports and printed materials, I checked out how they both corroborated and supplemented each other.

There were many stories about those *hasidim* and their Rabbis, which indeed contained a lot of important information about the history of hasidism. However, many of the materials were written without any order or methodology and without adequately checking out their sources. The wheat and chaff were mixed together. My task as the researcher was to sort out the wheat from the chaff.

I used a scholarly approach, based on sources from *hasidim*, *mitnagdim*, and *maskilim*. Trying to shed light on the subject, I checked out those sources very carefully. Among the important sources were the letters of Rabbi Yosef Levinshtein of Serotsek, who was personally acquainted with all of the great hasidic masters in Poland.

Other sources were: *Ramatayim Tsofim* by Rabbi Shmuel Sheinover, a brilliant student of Rabbi Simcha Bunim; the original letter of Rabbi Eliezer Tsvi Charlap, the Rabbi of Tiktin, which was generously given to me by the scholar, Rabbi Yaacov Moshe Charlap of Jerusalem, and illustrates the outlook of the *mitnagdim* toward the *hasidim* of Pshis'cha. Important material also was found in the *haskalah* literature of Yitschak Meezs, and in Polish-Jewish history books written in Hebrew, Yiddish and Polish, which I used to shed light on the political and economic conditions of Polish Jewry during this period.

Following this approach, I wrote the book on Rabbi Yaakov Yitschak from Pshis'cha, *Ha-*

Yehudi HaKadosh, and my current book on Rabbi Simcha Bunim from Pshis'cha, which is a continuation of the first book. The book was first published in a serialized version in the monthly journal, "Sinai," but this present output includes in the text footnotes and much additional material such as testimonies, the picture of Rabbi Simcha Bunim, a photograph of his handwriting, and supplementary stories and sayings at the end of the book.

In addition, the picture of Rabbi Simcha Bunim of Pshis'cha is found in the Bergson collection of the Warsaw congregation. It was drawn by an artist in the Berko and Tamar Bergson household in Warsaw who drew the two great hasidic masters in Poland, Rabbi Simcha Bunim of Pshis'cha and Rabbi Meir Halevi of Apta, when they were in Warsaw. The picture was also approved by the older *hasidim* who were acquainted with Rabbi Simcha Bunim.

The photograph of the Simcha Bunim letter was taken from the book, *The Rabbi of Simcha*, by R. M. N. HaCohen, from P. Z. Glickman of Lodz (1930). The letter remains in Lodz with one of the grandsons of Rabbi Moshe Nechemia HaCohen, the head of the court in Vurteh, Poland, who was the recipient of the letter and a former student of Rabbi Simcha Bunim.

I extend my thanks to the Rav Kook Institute: to the leaders, Rabbi Y. L. HaCohen Fishman and Mr. Yitschak Verfel, to the *tvunah* committee, and to the scholarly Torah organization. My thanks also to Mr. Yehudah in Tel Aviv, the son of Rabbi Avraham Yaacov Gurman and grandson of Rabbi Simcha Bunim of Pshis'cha, who made it possible for me to publish this book. May it be a blessing for everyone.

Tel Aviv, 1944
H. M. Rabinovits

Introduction

THE FATHERS OF HASIDISM IN POLAND AND THE REASONS FOR ITS DISSEMINATION

The three main streams of hasidism. The brothers, Rabbis Shmuel & Pinchas Horowitz, Rabbi Uziel of Yezlish, and the Rabbi from Berditchev. The ban on hasidism in Brodi. The defence of R. Shmuel Horowitz. The debate in Praga. The defaming writers. The political and economic causes for the dissemination of hasidism. The Magid of Koznits, his life and his teaching. The righteousness of R. Moshe Leib from Sasov. The Seer of Lublin.

There were three spiritual centers of hasidism. The Ukrainian (Vohlin, Podolya) stream was the first and most original. It was the cradle of hasidism and the center of activity of its founder, Rabbi Israel (Besht) (1698-1760) and his earliest disciples. In Ukraine, the learning of Talmud had never reached a high level and hasidism adapted to this situation. It served the broad masses and was popular. The books of the disciples of the Besht, the Magid of Mezeritch (1704-1772), Rabbi Yaakov Yosef of Polnoya

(1710-1784), and Rabbi Ephraim of Sadilkov, indicate a wide range of basic hasidic subjects, such as *tsimtsum* (contracting spiritually), *ha'alot nitsotsot* (the elevation of holy sparks), *bitul hayesh* (negation of the self in prayer), *y'chudim* (meditations on the oneness of G-d), and the like. Their content essentially focused on studies which were on a popular level.

The second stream, which took place in Bielorus (White Russia), included a greater degree of scholarship. In contrast to that of Ukrainian hasidism, Rabbi Shneur Zalman of Liadi (1745-1813), the founder of the Chabad *hasidim*, was a brilliant scholar in Talmud and profoundly learned in hasidism as well. He was the author of The *Shulchan Aruch Ha-Rav* and creator of *The Tanya*. Therefore, the stream of Chabad was a blend of Talmudic erudition and hasidism.

The third stream, the latest of them all, was the stream from Galicia, Poland. R. Elimelech from Lizhensk (1717-1787), was considered to be its creator. Their literature did not reflect an exploration of the academic concepts that had been already founded by their predecessors, who were the original path-finders. Rather, they were more concerned with the implementation of the teachings of hasidism. In this stream of Polish hasidic literature, frequent topics covered were: fervent prayer, social justice, love of friends, awe & love of G-d, communion with G-d, humility, and the greatness of a *tsadik*.

The war between the *hasidim* and the *mitnagdim* was not as strong in Poland as it was in Lithuania. There, the forceful personality of the Gaon of Vilna, along with all his rabbinic followers, stood at the head of the big debate opposing hasidism. However, in Poland, such an opposing personality who could stem the hasidic tide was not found. Those who fought against hasidism in Poland were lay leaders and rabbis of a lower level.

In contrast, there were two brilliant scholars in Poland, Rabbi Shmuel and Rabbi Pinchas Horowitz, among the founders of hasidism who defended the movement with courage and vigour. They converted many people and, to their credit, it spread widely.

There were four leaders of Polish hasidism who laid the cornerstone of the movement. The first leader was Rabbi Shmuel Horowitz, (c.1726-1778) who was one of the students of the Rabbi Dov Ber of Mezeritch. He was the rabbi in the city of Riszhvil in the interior of Poland. Many of the great ones of hasidism in Poland emerged from the Riszhvil *yeshivah*, i.e. Rabbi Yaacov Yitschak of Lublin (1745-1815), known as the Seer, Rabbi Israel, the Magid from Koznits (1740-1814), Rabbi Moshe Leib of Sasov (1745-1807) and others. From this little town, Rabbi Shmuel was accepted as the Rabbi and Head of the Court in Nicholsberg.

The second leader was his brother, Rabbi

Pinchas Horowitz (1730-1805), the author of *Hafla-ah (The Wonder)*, who was accepted as the Rabbi of Frankfurt on Main. The Magid of Mezeritch said about both brothers that "he found a house full of candles except they were not lit. He threw one spark on them and it lit all of them and from that spark came a great light." It was these two brothers who lit the candle of hasidism in Poland. Their brilliance in Torah and their elevated piousness protected them from attacks by the *mitnagdim*. Due to their influence, hasidism was turned into a popular movement and was embraced by the common folk. Jews by the thousands, from the most scholarly to the most simple folk in Poland, embraced hasidism.

Apart from the two brothers, Rabbis Shmuel and Pinchas Horowitz, hasidism was spread by two other rabbis. Rabbi Levi Yitschak of Berdichev, (1740-1810), a native of the interior part of Poland, was rabbi in the city of Zlichov till the year 1785. He drew large masses of Polish Jewry because of his great love for Israel and his righteousness. The other rabbi was Rabbi Uziel of Yezlish, one of the great students of the Magid of Mezeritch, who came from one of the most distinguished families in Poland. He became the rabbi in the towns of Rizhvil, Ostrovtsi, and Novidbor. He wrote the books *Ets Ha-daat (The Tree of Knowledge*, Warsaw 1863), *Tiferet Uziel, (The Splendour of Uziel)* and wrote on different tractates of the Talmud and hasidism. He was very knowledgeable in Torah and also known for his righteousness.

These four giants of hasidism, all of them students of the Magid of Mezeritch, were greatly learned in Torah and faith and they were able to counter all the attacks of the *mitnagdim*. The scholarship in Talmud of the four leaders, their extreme piousness and their great love for the people Israel were the best guarantees that they would not stray from the accepted path of Torah. Therefore, Jews of Poland joined the hasidic movement in droves.

From the point of view of the *mitnagdim*, they saw that hasidism was winning the hearts and minds of the people and the *mitnagdim* felt they had to pursue and purge them from their midst. Thus the courts in Brodi and Krakow, excommunicated all the followers of hasidism. They described the situation in the following way:

> *New followers of hasidism came from nearby and they did not leave a footprint in the sea of Talmud. Young people, tender in years, dared to build a bima (podium) for themselves, to change the traditional versions of chanting, to form groups, to pray while speaking arrogantly. They made strange movements, twisting their heads, spreading and clapping their hands, and waving their hands like wings of a stork, and bowing their heads in*

the prayer worship service.

And they said, "The Talmud is not the important thing." But Rabbi Shmuel Horowitz and his followers were not silent. Rabbi Shmuel in an open proclamation said,

> *I heard and felt anger right down to my gut about a voice calling out in the community, a voice to degrade true believers who follow the traditions of the Ari, of blessed memory, saying, G-d forbid, that they went and threw off from their necks the yoke of Torah and service to G-d.*

He admonished the community of Brodi that they had become a branch which was strictly adhering to the dictates of the people of Vilna. Rabbi Shmuel continued,

> *Pure nonsense flows out of their mouths as they defame true believers. On the contrary, all the people who have joined the hasidim engage themselves in Torah study even in their spare time and dedicate themselves to the worship of the heart, which is true prayer. Do we not all have one Father? Why do we betray one another? The people should not be divided in half. It is appropriate for you to fix this crack so that this will not happen to the dispersed flock.*

As long as Rabbi Shmuel and Rabbi Pinchas Horowitz were in Poland, they were able to defend hasidism and people heeded their words. However, when they traveled to the lands west of Poland, libellous writers, such as Yisrael Leible, author of *Zamir Aritsim (Singer of Tyrants)*, and a number of rabbis, once again emerged, opposing hasidism.

An especially famous debate about hasidism occurred in Praga, a city adjacent to Warsaw. Rabbi Yitschak Benyamin Volf, son of Rabbi Betsalel of Volkah and the uncle of Rabbi Simcha Bunim, lived there and was successfully engaged in spreading hasidism. Rabbi Avraham Katsnellenboig, head of the court of Brisk in Lithuania, and a zealous *mitnaged*, came to one of the synagogues in Praga to publicly debate with Rabbi Levi Yitschak of Berditchev on the essence of hasidism. He was accompanied in his war on hasidism by the well-known hater of hasidism, Yisrael Leible, who printed there the book, *Vikuach (Debate)*, and *Kivrot Hata'ava (Graves of Lust)*, in which he sharply denounced all the leaders of hasidism in Poland. But even these libellous writings, as well as the rabbinic excommunication and attacks by the *maskilim*, did not lessen the influence of the *tsadikim* in Poland.

The political unrest in the country also contributed to the strengthening of hasidism. After the death of the Polish king, Yahn Sovsky, c. 1756, unsettling days ensued and the unrest increased. The neighbouring countries coveted Poland and plotted to split and annex Poland. The imminent collapse of the Polish kingdom and its partition among the neighbouring nations, Russia, Prussia and Austria seemed apparent. The Kings, August II and August III, 1753-1787, were too weak and were unable to maintain any state discipline. The land was given to each regional noble to rule. Among the nobles, bribery and serving the interests of the neighbouring kingdoms increased.

The situation in general among the Jews who were subjugated by this aristocracy, became unbearable. The prevalence of the blood libel had increased to a terrifying extent. The Jesuits and priests felt strong enough to make up libels with impunity and to instigate *pogroms* (riots) and defame the name of Israel. High taxes, fees, and the exploitation of their possessions had impoverished them. In one of the journals of the times, they wrote,

> *We nearly despaired. Our hope was lost and the status of our community was ruined. It was calamity upon calamity. We could find no rest. With so many woes in this world relating to the false libels and all the blood letting, and there was a need for much money for bribes and gifts to save the remnant of our people who were still in prison. Apart from all this, the*

*tyrannical nobles with their drawn
swords, the priests, monasteries and
cloisters were choking us financially
to the tune of thousands and tens of
thousands of rubles. Each day they
oppressed and burdened us with
more and more costs that were
arbitrary additions and not even
according to the law. These usurers
came plotting to kill us.*

In 1724, the Jewish self-governing body,
the Council of the Four Lands, [1] that had been in
existence for hundreds of years was abolished.
City by city, state by state, its leaders and rabbis
who had functioned within the framework of
this excellent organization of Jewry which
provided law and a regulatory role, became
extinct. This situation made it possible for
hasidism to spread because it diffused the
creation of any serious obstacles.

With the first partition of Poland in 1772,
the political situation continued to worsen. The
Jewish community was divided between the
governments of Russia, Prussia and Austria. The
Jewish center that remained in the interior of
Poland experienced the agony of a kingdom that
was about to expire. In the year 1793, the second
partition occurred. Once again the unity within

---

[1] Council of the Four Lands - founded at the end of the fifteenth
century, a supreme council which controlled the Jewish activities
of Great and Little Poland and the provinces of Lemburg and
Volynia. G.L.

the Jewish community disintegrated.

Only in Lithuania did it meet resistance from the scholarly Rabbi Eliyahu, who had also encouraged the communities of Brodi and Krakow to excommunicate *hasidim*. However, the *mitnagdim* lacked the power of a recognized central authority like the former Council of the Four Lands. The Frankist movement and the dispute between Rabbi Yaacov Emdin and Rabbi Yonatan Evshits had already created divisiveness and the disintegration of a unified greater Israel, thereby leading to the weakening of the authority of the rabbis.

Hasidim used every means of publicity available to spread their teachings among the oppressed masses, who wished to be liberated from the heavy yoke of the *parnasim* (religious administrators) and leaders of the community. Ordinary people were thirsty for the word of G-d found in the prayers of the early *hasidim*, for the joy of life, for melodious song, for the love of Israel and the early Polish *tsadikim*. Their teachings blurred the division between the learned and the ignorant and emphasized the person's initial intention with a focus on Torah of the heart.

Hasidism reached the climax of its development with the appearance of three great leaders: the Rabbi Yisrael from Koznits, Rabbi Moshe Leib from Apta-Sasov, and Rabbi Yaacov Yitschak Horowitz, known as the Seer of Lublin. Each one emphasized a special and distinct path.

Rabbi Moshe Leib excelled in love of Israel; The Magid of Kosnits focused on prayer and brilliant erudition; The Seer's direction took him through the Holy Spirit to wonders and visions. The fruit of all their promotional publicizing led to the quick expansion of hasidism in Poland. The common people, the great rabbis and famous scholars who came from near and far, all came to accept the authority of this new movement.

The Magid of Koznits, 1740-1814, was born in Ostrovy. His father, Rabbi Shabtai became a book-binder in his later years. According to a well-known hasidic legend, he was said to have derived his strength through a blessing he received from the Besht. In his youth, the Magid studied in the *yeshivot* of Poland with the great ones of that generation. After his marriage in the town of Pshis'cha, he grew close to the scholar, Rabbi Shmuel Hurvitz, who was then the rabbi in Ryzsvil. The latter convinced him to join with the *hasidim* and to study hasidic teachings directly from Dov Ber, the Magid of Mezeritch and Rabbi Elimelech of Lyzhensk.

The Magid of Koznits was also known as a "Wonder-Maker". From the length and breadth of Poland, Jews, non-Jews and even nobles, such as Yosef Ponitovsky and Adam Chrotorisky, flocked to him. In Polish sources and memoirs of the time, the Magid is mentioned with high esteem and great admiration. He was also very supportive of the Polish liberation movement and the Emperor Napoleon, who founded the

Duchy of Warsaw and promised to return the German and Russian parts that were torn from Poland, and renew the former Polish kingdom.

Physically, the Magid was a very thin and frail person who spent most of his days in bed, swaddled in pillows to keep him warm. Sometimes, because of his physical weakness, he was not able to come to the study hall and he would be carried there by his *hasidim*. However, his great weakness did not hinder the power of his personal prayers that were said in a strong voice, with fervour and deep communion with G-d. A similar thing occurred at mealtimes. In spite of the fact that he hardly ate anything, he used to deliver his teachings in such a loud strong voice that he left his listeners in awe. He was dedicated to the study of Torah all his years. Day and night he used to teach in the *yeshivah*, engage in Talmud, *Kabalah* and hasidism, and correspond regularly with the great scholars and sages of his generation. Even his most bitter opponent, the author of *Zamir Aritsim*, in spite of his diatribes that the Magid was impoverishing the people, had to acknowledge that the Magid was a learned man and his faith was his sole occupation.

The second leader, who was a major figure in disseminating hasidism, was Rabbi Moshe Leib of Sasov who lived in the city of Apta in his youth. He, too, like the Magid of Koznits, was a student of Rabbi Shmuel of Nickolsberg and also engaged in Torah, writing new insights in Talmud and hasidism. However, the essence of his fame was in "the love of Israel". He excelled in deeds of loving kindness and charity to the oppressed and the poor. He was like a father to all the orphans and widows and always worried about how to fill their needs. He used to say, "One who can not suck out the blood of the plagues and the boils of the children of Israel has not yet attained half the love of Israel." A famous legend about this *tsadik* is as follows:

Once, on the eve of *Yom HaKippurim*, he was late in coming to the synagogue to pray *Kol Nidrei*. They searched for him and found him in a house holding a crying baby in his arms. The baby had been left there by its mother who had gone to pray. The *tsadik* proceeded to put the baby to sleep with a lullaby.

Rabbi Moshe Leib was especially engaged in the *mitzvah* of *pidyon shvuim*, the redemption of the captives. He sought to redeem the tenants of estates who did not have sufficient money to make their payments to the nobles. This same characteristic warmth and love of Israel and joy of performing *mitsvot* permeated all his teachings. These were compiled in his book, *Likutei Ramal, Collections of Rabbi Moshe Leib*. *Hasidim* tell wonders about his prayers that were steeped in *devekut* and fervour and made a strong impression on all observers. Many thousands of Jews, especially the highly enthusiastic youth, became *hasidim* under the influence of his charisma. Among his students was Rabbi Yaacov Yitschak, known as the "Yehudi HaKadosh", (the Holy Jew). Under the influence of Rabbi Moshe Leib, the Yehudi who had been a *mitnaged*, became a fervent *hasid* and went on to found a new school in hasidism in Pshis'cha.

The third leader among the extraordinary men who led the hasidic movement in Poland, was Rabbi Yaacov Yitschak Horowitz, known as "the Seer of Lublin" for the wonders he performed. He, too, was a student of the Magid of Mezeritch and of Rabbi Elimelech of Lyzhensk. Initially, he lived in Lintsot, Galicia, later settling in Lublin.

Rabbi Horowitz made a very significant impact on Polish Judaism. His followers grew exponentially into the tens of thousands and the great rabbis of the times gathered around him and became imbued with the spirit of hasidism. The "Court of Lublin" became the creative studio in which the very soul of hasidism was fashioned. Almost all its leaders and administrators were students of the Seer. The leader of the *mitnagdim* who opposed the Seer was Rabbi Azriel of Lublin, often referred to as "Iron Head" because of his sharp-witted manner of speaking. The *mitnagdim* directed all their arrows against the Seer, but they could not stop the spirit of the times. In spite of their pursuit, hasidism reached the apex of its development at this time and imprinted its signature on the cultural and economic lives of Polish Jewry.

Pshis'cha hasidism branched out from these roots, i.e. the 'courts' of these *tsadikim*. The transmitters of this hasidism were Rabbi Yaacov Yitschak of Pshis'cha, known as "the Yehudi HaKadosh," and Rabbi Simcha Bunim of Pshis'cha. It is the life and teachings of Rabbi Simcha Bunim to whom the following chapters are dedicated.

Chapter 1

YOUTH

His parents. The greatness of his father and the distinguished lineage of his mother. His city of birth. His early education. R. Yermiah of Mattersdorf. The yeshivot in Moravia & Bohemia. R. Mordechai Banet. His marriage. His growing attraction to hasidism.

Rabbi Simcha Bunim was born in Pshis'cha (Polish: Przysuscha), Poland, about 1765 (5525). His father, Rabbi Tsvi, was a well-known *magid*, an itinerant preacher, from Vadislav. Rabbi Tsvi used to travel throughout most of the cities of Poland, Hungary, and Bohemia, explaining and interpreting Torah in many different synagogues. Because of his knowledge of Torah and his great preaching skills, the rabbis of these communities often invited him to their synagogues and helped to support him. He used to expound on such topics as repentance, humility, relationships between man and G-d, and man and man. He often seasoned his sermons with parables and medieval philosophic passages and his influence grew among the listeners of his sermons.

Yechezkel Lando, the author of *Hanoda B'yehudah*, wrote, "Whenever we heard that he

1

had visited a community in which he had expounded, the rabbis sang his praises and we all heard of his fame. He was a great *magid*, and expounded well to his people. His speech was pleasant, flowing beautifully from his lips, charming and sweet as honey and nectar, and when he admonished them, he did it with great sensitivity." The rabbis, Yitschak HaLevi, the head of the court in Krakov, Elazar in Kalim, and Yermiah, the Rav in Mattersdorf, spoke about him in a similar vein.

Rabbi Tsvi, who had a close relationship with Rabbi Yermiah, wrote, "This Shabbat he visited with us here…and I was kept very entertained. I made his acquaintance when I was in the state of Poland and knew that G-d filled him with the spirit of wisdom." Two books of Rabbi Tsvi's sermons, *Asara L'maya* and *Erets Hatsvi*, still remain.

The mother of Simcha Bunim, Sara, was the daughter of the Rav Betsalel from Zolkvah, author of the book, *B'shem Betsalel*. She was descended from a distinguished family of rabbis who were greatly learned in Torah, and who came from an eminent line of scholars going back to Rabbi Joel Sirkes, the "Bach" of Blessed memory.

The city of Vadislav, one of the oldest Jewish communities in Poland, was a place in which a great number of rabbis served in the study of Torah and where Torah study was also widely practiced by ordinary people. One even found scholars among business men and lay people. This environment of Torah study and the erudition and wisdom of his father greatly influenced Simcha Bunim. He learned in the local *cheder* in his city until he was 10 years old. According to the tales of some of his *hasidim*, he also excelled in Talmud in his youth.

Rabbi Tsvi nurtured in his son the love of rational learning and common sense. His father wrote in one of his books, "I didn't bring into this essay any sermons too biting, but rather I always taught in simple and gentle ways. Just as Isaiah wrote *Laacov L'maysharay*, I used a built-in basis for advancement that would be compatible with their hearts so that the human mind could agree and affirm them." These words of his father were a guiding light for Simcha Bunim. Rabbi Tsvi's personality and his focus on common sense, his ability to expound, and his grasp of reality, were his son's role models. Rabbi Simcha Bunim recalled him with great admiration and often quoted his father's words.

His father often told him stories about other countries in Europe and about the Jews who lived there and their customs. At that time, there were many great *yeshivot* in the states of Hungary, Moravia, and Bohemia. In all the places where Jews settled, whether they were large or small communities, there were rabbis and many young men engaged in Torah. The researcher, Isaac Hersh Veiss, described these *yeshivot* in his *Memoirs*. He stated that their size depended on the number of wealthy businessmen in the congregation, and other members of the community who could sponsor and support these students. Through the good will of businessmen and others, their needs were partially provided. When that which they provided was not enough for most of their needs, even poor Jews shared their bread with the young men with love and a willing spirit because they were so passionate to do *tsedaka*. The deeds of the young men were wondrously good as was the dedication of their souls to the study of Torah. It felt easy for a poor young man to live all week on a little bread, hardly any water, sitting in hunger and studying Torah day and night. Neither poverty nor any other kind of need had the power to deter them from their studies. Those young men who succeeded in procuring food for themselves, such as one meal a day, considered themselves happy.

His father's stories awakened in Simcha Bunim the desire to travel so that he could further his Torah studies. Therefore, his father, Rabbi Tsvi, the Magid, sent Simcha Bunim to the states of Hungary and Moravia to study with the rabbis who were his friends.

Rabbi Tsvi wanted his son to be educated in Rabbi Yermiah's rational way of teaching *halacha*. In Mattersdorf, Simcha Bunim studied in the famous *yeshivah* with Rabbi Yermiah. Simcha Bunim loved his teacher, the great Rabbi Yermiah and diligently continued his studies of

4

Talmud with him for several years.

Rabbi Yermiah, a native of Poland, became famous in different communities as a great scholar. He was called to serve as rabbi and head of the *yeshivah* in Mattersdorf, Hungary, in 1770 (5530). He headed the *yeshivah* for 28 years and educated thousands of students. In the year 1798 (5558), he published his book, *Modaah Raba* in Lvov. In that same year, he was accepted as the rabbi in Santov. He died there in 1805 (5565).

In Hungary, Simcha Bunim also studied in Nikolsburg at the *yeshiva* of the *gaon*, Rabbi Mordechai Banet, who was the head of all the states of Monrovia. The influence of this rabbi on R. Simcha Bunim was huge and he always mentioned his name, too, with great admiration.

Rabbi Mordechai Banet who lived from 1753 to 1829 (5513-5589) was one of the great scholars of his time, together with Rabbi Moshe Sofer *(Chatam Sofer)*, Rabbi Yaacov from Lysa, the author of *Chavat Da'at*, and Rabbi Akiva Eiger from Pozna. They fought a vigorous war against assimilation and reform. They also inspired those who fought against the rigid orthodox adherence to the 'letter of the law' in the name of Jerusalem and who treated the words in the *siddur* as if they were set in stone. The way of learning in Rabbi Banet's *yeshiva* was rational, probing deeply, without *pilpul* (quibbling over inconsequentia). Students were taught primarily from the books of Rambam which had a major influence on Simcha Bunim from Pshis'cha. It was customary to study on a daily basis *Yad Chazakah (With a Strong Hand)* of Rambam.

Rabbi Mordechai Banet's knowledge of the Hebrew language, especially its grammar, was formidable, as well as his knowledge of the secular sciences such as mathematics and philosophy. He was very precise in his use of grammar and had a deep understanding of the wisdom of the holy tongue, as well as his great learning of Talmud. He was also very learned and familiar with books that explored and probed the philosophy of religion, such as *Moreh N'vuchim (Guide to the Perplexed)*, and *Ikarim*, and the like. According to the stories of his son, Avraham, who wrote his father's biography, he also knew the German language and had a breadth of knowledge of several other secular subjects. He never rebuked his sons for learning the language of the surrounding peoples or studying other books of wisdom. Rather he encouraged his sons not to avoid them. Rabbi Simcha Bunim's knowledge of languages and his inclination for medieval philosophy can be directly attributed to the influence of the *gaon*, Rabbi Mordechai Banet.

Rabbi Mordechai Banet had an outstanding personality, and was seen as having achieved the perfection of the *midot* and scholarship. He personified the virtues of Judaism. A. H. Weiss, a researcher of his generation, in describing Rabbi Banet, said:

> *He was made holy even from the*

time he was in the womb, with wondrous natural abilities, a wise heart, profound knowledge, and an incredibly powerful memory. R. Mordechai Banet came from poor people, but, with the years, this son of poor people became unique in his generation. There isn't a mouth that can speak enough about the acts of loving kindness that he did for the poor of his people. His earnings were meagre. The earnings allotted to him didn't reach half the value of his greatness. In spite of all this, he supported the poor freely with what he had, with a willing heart showing no difference to Jews or non-Jews.

The pure awe of G-d, the dedication of his soul to Torah, deeds of justice, love of mercy, the behaviour of modesty, all these were traits that he acquired by perseverance. He was very determined to keep himself from unwillingly doing that which was frowned upon in the eyes of G-d and man. In his old age, Rabbi Simcha Bunim often used to recall those inspiring days of traveling in the *yeshivot* of Hungary and Moravia.

After Rabbi Simcha Bunim returned from Hungary, he married Rivkah, the daughter of R. Moshe Oharoreger from Bandin. Rivkah, known as "the Rebbitsin from Pshis'cha", fulfilled the traditional role of a wife of a rabbi. She was known for her charity, her good traits, and truly fulfilled the ideal of an *eshet chayil*, "woman of valour". She always stood beside her husband and was his right hand.

For several years, he was supported by his father-in-law so that he could dedicate himself to the study of Talmud without any worries. It was during this early phase in his development that he began to grow closer to the hasidic movement. In spite of the fact that his father, Rabbi Tsvi, was a fierce opponent, Rabbi Bunim began to behave in hasidic fashion, praying with fervour, and striving for ethical perfection.

It appears that the influence of his mother's brother, Rabbi Yitschak Benyamin Volf from Praga,[1] was bringing him closer to hasidism. This uncle was one of the early rabbis who spread hasidism energetically and with much devotion. After Rabbi Simcha Bunim's return from Hungary, he studied with his uncle in Praga for a period of time. It was at this time that he traveled to the great *tsadikim* in Poland, such as Rabbi Moshe Leib from Sasov-Apt and the Magid, Rabbi Israel from Koznits.

Rabbi Bunim had seen directly with his own eyes the decline of Judaism and the growth of assimilation in Hungary and in Germany. Assimilation was causing the destruction of a number of long standing communities. He began to see hasidism in general, and *tshuvah* and

---

[1] The city adjacent to Warsaw. A suburb.

spiritual uplift in particular, as the only way to save Judaism.

Although the great leaders of Hungary, such as Rabbi Yermiah from Mattersdorf and Rabbi Mordechai Banet, were opposed to hasidism, they did not persecute them as the rabbis of Lithuania did. Therefore, the transition to hasidism did not generate a difficult psychological crisis for Rabbi Simcha Bunim. At this point, he aligned himself with the leaders of hasidism in spite of the limitations of his soul and the inexperience of his youth.

Chapter 2

HIS ADVANCING HASIDISM AND INTELLIGENCE

Bunim's friendship with the Magid of Koznits. Shmuel Zvitkove and his deed of charity. Dov and Tamar Bergson. His position vis-à-vis the Bergsons. His commercial relationships. His continued learning European languages. His examination to be a pharmacist. His engagement with hasidism and with the Seer of Lublin.

Before long, the financial support from his father-in-law ceased and Rabbi Simcha Bunim was forced to face the realities of the practical financial world. He had to seek a source of livelihood. Hasidism came to his rescue. Rabbi Simcha Bunim became one of the fervent *hasidim* of Rabbi Moshe Leib from Sassov and the Magid of Koznits, who regarded him highly and made him his confidante. In his old age, he still felt the strong influence of the Magid, whom he always recalled with great admiration and honour.

Through the Magid of Koznits, Rabbi Simcha Bunim grew close to the wealthy house of the Warsavian, Berko Dov Zonenberg-Bergson, and his wife, Tamar. Berko was the son of the philanthropist Shmuel Zvitkover. Shmuel was considered the wealthiest man among the Jews of Poland and was known and respected in the Polish king's court and among the great aristocrats and ministers of the State. The Polish government transferred contracts and monopolistic businesses to him.

He is especially known for his role during the time of the Polish Revolt of 1794, known as the "Revolt of Kosciosko". The Jews of Warsaw fought together with the Poles against the Russian armies under the command of Barak Yoselovitch, who founded the Jewish Brigade. However, in spite of the courage of the Poles and the Jews, the Russians were victorious. Fifteen thousand Poles together with approximately 600 of the Jewish Brigade were slain on the ramparts of Praga, and in the streets of Warsaw. Many of them fell into the waters of the Vistula River.

There is a legend that after the battles, the Russians were still in the throes of killing and decimating all the residents of the city of Warsaw. R. Shmuel Zvitkover sat in his courtyard, with two barrels by his side; one was full of gold coins and the second one contained silver coins. He sent out a proclamation to the Cossacks, that for each live person, he would give a gold ruble…for each dead one, a silver one. The Russian army came in droves to R. Shmuel to receive the coins, bringing with them the living and the dead. In a short time they emptied the two barrels. And thus he saved hundreds of people from death.

Berko Dov Bergson, the son of the above mentioned Rabbi Shmuel Zvitkover became the head of the family. The famous twentieth century French-Jewish philosopher, Bergson, was a descendent of Berko Dov Bergson. Berko, like his father, was a government contractor and extremely rich, and, like him, was also engaged in the welfare of Polish Jewry. Till 1818 he was head of the Warsaw community and most of the community affairs were decided by him.

In the year 1816, Bergson traveled to St. Petersburg as head of a Jewish delegation. He met with the Minister responsible for educational matters to complain about the dissemination of "blood libel" propaganda that was rampant in Poland at that time. He talked about the cruel stubbornness of the bureaucrats and governors of the regions, who believed in these libels and who were punishing Jews. It was largely through his efforts that the minister issued a firm order to all the governors of the regions. From that day on, he declared that they should not pay attention to all these libels and that if they were to continue their actions, the state would punish the libellers with the full strength of the law.

Berko's wife, Tamar, was very well-known for her many charitable works and her help to poor people. The hasidic movement succeeded to draw unto itself this rich couple as benefactors. In time, they became fervent *hasidim*. They were eager to visit the Magid of Koznits and the Seer of Lublin. Tamar Bergson supported several courts of *tsadikim* and important *hasidim* and often appointed them as clerks and managers in her stores. Rabbi Simcha Bunim from Pshis'cha, was one of those managers along with Rabbi Yitschak of Vorkah, who was the spiritual father of the Dynasty "Alexander" in Poland.

Rabbi Simcha Bunim from Pshis'cha was responsible for handling Bergson's forestry dealings. He arranged the transportation of wood products to the port of Danzig and then on to barges for shipping. From time to time he accompanied the merchandise to the great Fair in Leipzig, Germany. These commercial relationships required him to know several European languages and he learned to speak Polish, German and Italian. He also wore European clothes, which he did not remove even after his return to Poland. He wore European clothes even in his entrance to the courts of the *tsadikim*.[2] Folk legends of the *hasidim* did not try to conceal the fact that Rabbi Simcha Bunim, while staying in the European cities, used to visit the theatre. He made friends with *maskelim*, and often played cards with those with whom he had commercial connections. In many ways he was a very modern and worldly man.

Some of his *hasidim* even tried to justify his behaviour. They said that by playing these

---

[2] European dress was in contrast to the long black coats worn by *hasidim*.

games with them, he inspired *maskilim* toward engaging in a transformative process which would prevent them from committing future sinful ways. Rabbi Simcha Bunim taught that to engage in the work of this world is truly G-d's way. He taught that one needs to connect the trials and tests of this world to a higher world. He said that to elevate them is the highest form of worship one can attain. "As a rule," his *hasidim* said, "...a righteous man is not spoiled, even in an impure place. Did not Avraham, our father, when he was in Egypt, not fall from his degree of holiness?" The *hasidim* saw that a great human being like Rabbi Simcha Bunim was the "good" that was in the theatre and not the "bad" that was within it. According to the words of his *hasidim*, he drew holy sparks from there.

Rabbi Bunim wanted to earn a living from a more honoured and useful profession, and so, after a time, he ceased his employment with the Bergson business. Although it wasn't widespread among Jews, especially among the ultra-orthodox, R. Bunim pursued studies in pharmacy. He traveled to Lvov and passed the examination by the "Committee for Medical Affairs", and received his certificate "Registered Pharmacist". In the desire to give their stamp of approval, some *hasidim* tell the story that the head examiner gave Rabbi Bunim money to buy a reference book for pharmacology. However, instead of buying the reference book with the money, he bought the book, the *Zohar*.

The pharmacy opened in Pshis'cha, which is in the region of Radom. Rabbi Simcha Bunim's pharmacy was known to the Polish aristocrats and to the doctors in the area, and he made a decent living. During the time of the Napoleonic wars, he supplied medicines for the French army. We do not know the precise dates of the length of time that he engaged in this profession. However by the year 1803 (5553), his signature was still found in the registry of the burial society in Pshis'cha, together with the signature of the Magid, Rabbi Avraham.

The city was the center of hasidism. The Magid of Koznits received his education there and, at that time, the Magid, Rabbi Avrahm, who was famous in his generation for his erudition, was also living in that city. In spite of his business in the pharmacy, he never stopped engaging in the study and practice of hasidism. Apart from his trips to Koznits and Apta, he was also drawn to Rabbi David from Lelov, a wonderful *tsadik*, whose life was dedicated to the love of Israel.

Rabbi Simcha Bunim's fame and greatness really became better known from the time he traveled to the Seer of Lublin. The Seer loved him very much and he was one of the most intimate of his *hasidim*. Rabbi Bunim became so close to the Seer that the Seer said, "Bunim, stay beside me, and I will invest you with the holy spirit from the world of atsilut." However, some of the Seer's closest *hasidim*, especially the Galicians, could not accept the fact that Rabbi Simcha Bunim was so close to the Seer, because he was still in the every day work-world as a pharmacist, and he had been engaged in daily commerce in the land of Germany, the center of the *maskilim*. Nevertheless, Rabbi Simcha Bunim was beloved by many of the *tsadikim* of his generation, for his lineage, his erudition, his many connections with the great ones of Hungary, his knowledge of languages, and his influence with the Bergson family.

Rabbi Simcha Bunim, together with the Bergsons, was lobbying in government circles to alleviate the negative decrees that were promulgated against the *hasidim*, under the influence of the *mitnagdim*. As a student of the scholar, Rabbi Mordechai Banet, who was broadly educated and had great common sense, Rabbi Simcha Bunim had a firm grasp of knowledge and an understanding of economic and political life. He was famous for his cleverness and oratorical abilities, great in knowledge of Torah and hasidism and in *Yir'at HaShamayim* (reverence and awe of G-d), and for having refined his ethical traits. All these characteristics elevated respect for Rabbi Simcha Bunim in the courts of Koznits and Lublin and made him a central personality and a strong influence in Polish hasidism.

Chapter 3

"HAYEHUDI HAKADOSH" AND HIS INFLUENCE ON RABBI SIMCHA BUNIM

Rabbi Yaacov from Pshis'cha. Populist hasidism and Pshis'cha-hasidism. Its similarity to Chabad. Polish writers on the economic conditions of the Jews. The controversy between the Seer and the Yehudi. The rise to greatness of Rabbi Simcha Bunim.

In the early days of Polish hasidism, a new star arose in the heavens, Rabbi Yaacov Yitschak Rabinowitz from Pshis'cha (1766-1814), who was also known as "HaYehudi HaKadosh", (the Holy Jew). Yaacov Yitschak Rabinowitz was born in the city of Przedborz. He studied in the *yeshivot* of Poland and was known for his great learning in Torah. He drew close to hasidism through the influence of Rabbi Moshe Leib from Apta and the *Chozeh*, the Seer of Lublin, and became one of the Seer's closest disciples. He was admired by all the young scholars, the elite of the *hasidim*.

The teachings of Polish hasidism were populist in nature. It adapted itself to the demands of the time and the needs of the people. They came to the *tsadik* seeking help for their material needs and a life that was filled with

17

sorrows, suffering, and the hardship of life in exile. Rabbi Yaacov Yitschak of Lublin, the Seer, one of the most famous of the populist *tsadikim* wrote, "The Holy One, Blessed Be He, transmits to every generation to interpret the Written and Oral Torah, so that each generation of *tsadikim* will interpret the Written Torah in their distinct way according to their own understanding, and according to that particular time in their era." He interpreted the verse, "They judged the people in all time" (Exodus 18 v.22) as meaning that they should decide the *halacha* according to the season and the time. He felt a *tsadik* had to be interested in the material conditions of the people and to try to improve their lot. The Seer interpreted "according to time" to mean that one was to give advice to the poor, to cure the sick, to apportion charity, to redeem prisoners from tyrannical Polish landowners. "Go and see about the well-being of the flock" (Genesis 37 v.14), wrote one of the populist *tsadikim*.

There were also great and good *tsadikim*, whose entire lives were directed only to the exaltation of His glory, Blessed be His Name, and they paid attention neither to the well-being of this world nor did they attempt to influence their own generation. However, the populist *tsadikim* felt that this approach was incorrect because it was incumbent on the *tsadikim* to look at the world below, this world, and to pay attention to the livelihood of Jews in order to see that their needs were being met. They believed strongly that the *tsadik* had an obligation to look after his brother, i.e. the flock of this world. The Rabbi of Lublin was always busy counselling, engaging in healing, and helping the masses of ordinary people, and often did not have time to devote himself to the spiritual questions of his young *hasidim*.

Meanwhile, many of the young *hasidim* were frustrated and did not find spiritual satisfaction in the wonders of the Seer. In contrast to the Seer's approach, HaYehudi did not demonstrate wonders and a holy spirit. He was opposed to the signs and wonders practiced by the Seer. Instead, he taught a purer kind of hasidism, bringing new insights into Torah and Talmud. These very different approaches created a major conflict between the *Chozeh* and the Yehudi.

Although he had been one of the students of the Seer of Lublin, the Yehudi eventually left him. He gathered around him learned and dedicated students. The Yehudi founded a new kind of hasidism; one focused more on personal redemption. His followers clung to their new rabbi with all their hearts. He advocated the continuation of one's education and an inner moral perfection, the love of Torah, intellectual understanding, and profound insight in Jewish ethics. However, the teachings of the Yehudi were only for the few select brilliant scholars who thought that the spiritual life was more important than the materialistic one. The Yehudi was vehemently opposed to the signs and wonders practiced by the Seer. He basically worried about the particular pathways of spiritual well-being that were being chosen by Polish Jewish scholars. First and foremost, he demanded from his *hasidim* consistent ethical behaviour, honesty, performing the *mitsvot* with intentionality and without any ulterior motive or turning to materialistic thought. He sought the underlying intention and emphasized it as a higher priority than the actual *mitsvah* itself. He was so concerned with intentionality that his *hasidim* delayed the time of prayer, which was contrary to the law of *halacha*. They explained their position saying that only a prayer with intention is desirable and that if there were not the proper intention at the fixed time, the prayer must be postponed.

This approach of emphasizing the importance of intentionality was similar to that of the hasidism of Chabad and was one of the pillars of the teachings of R. Schneur Zalman from Liadi, who advanced hasidism to a higher cultural and intellectual level. R. Schneur Zalman taught a more profound approach to hasidism— one which had philosophic depth and was congruent with those of the scholars of Bielorus. They were totally opposed to any signs and wonders.

The Chabad *tsadik* saw his task as being one of a spiritual guide to a select class of *yeshivah* students. The materialistic helping and the healing of the masses of people were not part of his agenda. Therefore, it is clear that the new teaching of the "Yehudi" was also intended for only a small number of young disciples, mostly bridegrooms who were still dependent on the in-law's support and who didn't have to worry about making a living.

Because of the harsh conditions and terrible poverty, the majority of people continued to travel mainly to populist *tsadikim* seeking some kind of relief from their material fate. A Polish writer, Antony Ostrovsky, described the Jewish situation in these words:

> *The fate of the Jews is dependent on the will of their rulers. They drive them from the villages to the cities and from small cities to big ones. In the cities, they are often driven from one street to another. They also control the number of families who are permitted to live in a neighbourhood and specify the conditions in which they are allowed to earn a living.*
>
> *In each place they degrade and humble them and don't let them live in peace. The powers that be never show any good will or desire to rescue them from their poverty. Many of them wander daily in search of a slice of bread. From small humble earnings, a Jew occasionally*

acquires 100-200 gold coins. With this amount, he becomes a peddler or a tavern keeper. As a peddler, he goes to a village, buys from a farmer a chicken, eggs, or a little grain. In exchange, he gives him a little salt or other food needs and returns to the city.

According to the words of another Polish writer, three quarters of the Polish Jews were found to be in dire poverty, lacking even bread. The very poor classes found comfort and encouragement in the hasidic movement—in the fervour of prayer and in pure faith. They would make a pilgrimage to the big centers of hasidism. While there, they earned a living for a few days on the *tsadik's* financial account and for a short period of time, they could forget their poverty and their terrible situation. The *tsadikim* were also engaged in acquiring funds for charity for the benefit of poor people, trying various ways to approach the few rich people, to employ poor *hasidim* in administration or other work. Having a letter of recommendation from one of the Polish *tsadikim* was very valuable.

The *tsadikim* also lobbied the government to cancel the many evil economic and religious decrees against the Jews that were current at that time. Rabbi Yitschak, from M'vorka, was especially famous for this and he attempted to convince the authorities to cancel the decrees of banishment from the villages, the prohibition to engage in tavern-keeping, and others. He frequently went to see Novosiltsov, who was the Russian governor of Poland at that time. Rabbi Yitschak died in 1848.

The religious controversy which arose between the Yehudi and the Seer of Lublin caused a split among Polish *hasidim*. On the side of the Seer stood the spokesmen from the Galician *hasidim*, like Rabbi Naftali Tsvi from Rovshits, Rabbi Mendeli from Rymanov, and Rabbi Tsvi from Zitschov. Other famous rabbis and *tsadikim* in Poland also supported him, such as Rabbi Meir from Apta, Rabbi Shimon from Zilchov, and others. In contrast to the Seer's support, those who gathered around the Yehudi were the scholars who were opposed to populist hasidism. At the head of the admirers of the Yehudi, stood Rabbi Simcha Bunim from Pshis'cha. He was completely dedicated to his new rabbi. The Yehudi made Pshis'cha his permanent residence and Rabbi Simcha Bunim used to go to the Yehudi every evening after he closed his pharmacy to study Torah.

He called his teacher "golden sheaves of wheat". Rabbi Simcha Bunim felt that all the parts of wheat—the chaff, the seeds, and the straw—were pure gold. So too, did he feel that the personality of the Yehudi was pure gold—without one iota of sin or transgression. The Yehudi likewise lauded his student, calling him "the point of my heart". It was his way of saying that he had transmitted to him all of his wisdom and that there was no one who understood him as well as Rabbi Simcha Bunim. Rabbi Simcha Bunim was his advisor and confidante in all matters and accompanied his rabbi on his trip to Rabbi Mendeli, in Rymanov, who stood ready to mediate between the Yehudi and the Seer. The Seer of Lublin and all his disciples knew that Rabbi Simcha Bunim was deeply involved and wholly committed to his rabbi. Because he played a key role in the controversy between these two major hasidic leaders, the Seer's disciples maintained a deep hatred toward him. When Rabbi Bunim was later made a leader of *hasidim*, they recollected his involvement in the controversy and tried to strip him of his honour and his leadership.

The days of leadership by the Yehudi were not long. This *tsadik* was physically very weak. He had afflicted himself by much fasting during his younger days, and had struggled with his health and weakened body for a long time, until his soul departed in the year 1814 (5574), while he was still a young man of forty-eight. The scholars, who could not abide the populist approach to hasidism, were left like sheep without a shepherd. Polish hasidism lost one of its greatest helmsmen. Although his son, Yerachmiel, and one of his students, Rabbi Abba from Nishderdt, took the place of the Yehudi, the days of the latter leadership were not very long. Led by Rabbi Mendeli from Kotsk, the Yehudi's student, the scholars sought another leader who would fit their spiritual yearnings. The only one to whom they could turn to replace the lofty position of the Yehudi was Rabbi Simcha Bunim.

The *hasidim* relate that the disciples came to ask Rabbi Simcha Bunim for advice about who should govern as *tsadik*. He answered them with a parable: A shepherd once fell asleep at noon and slept until midnight. While he slept, the sheep were grazing to their hearts content. When he woke up, he was disturbed, startled, and very anxious about the well being of the flock. However, when he got up from the grass, he looked around him and observed that the skies were clear, the moon and the stars were sparkling radiantly, the air was fresh, and all the flock were standing beside a pleasantly gurgling brook in the quiet of the night. A prayer of thanks to G-d burst forth from his heart and he said: "Our Father in Heaven, what shall I give you in exchange for your abundant loving kindness? What am I but a poor shepherd. How can I thank You? In this way only will I shepherd and guard them, like the pupil of my eye from this day forth." Rabbi Simcha Bunim added, "If they will find a faithful shepherd like this, take him to be your Rabbi." When his students heard his beautiful parable, they arose from their places, with Rabbi Abba from Nishderdt at their head, and installed him in the position of the *tsadik*, accepting his authority.

Chapter 4

THE PHARMACIST WHO BECAME THE RABBI

Lublin and Pshis'cha. The hasidic youth movement. Understanding and research. Disparagement of the active commandments. War against pride. Overcoming superficial might. The conflict between Pshis'cha and the rest of the hasidim. The Pshis'cha delegation to the wedding in Ostila. The victory.

While Rabbi Simcha Bunim held the position of the Yehudi in 1815, his goal was to expand on his rabbi's teachings and to distil from them ultimate conclusions. Rabbi Bunim wanted to produce *hasidim* of deep understanding, thoroughly immersed in essential Jewish inwardness, and enveloped in sheer awe. They infused all their deeds with the elevated knowledge of one's innermost Jewish self and distanced themselves from any material ulterior motives or from pride, honour and money. Pshis'cha hasidism focused primarily on inner spirituality. The prayer of a poor person which is said in innocence and in fervour is important in the Heavens, but in Pshis'cha, they emphasized *chochma*, wisdom and *da'at*, knowledge. It was a hasidism of *binah*, understanding. He used to say, "Whereas populist hasidism concerns itself only with the poor, both materially and spiritually, I say in the verse, 'Say to wisdom, You are my sister, and call understanding a kinswoman.' (Proverbs 7:4) One is not poor except in knowledge." This saying incorporates the difference between Pshis'cha and Lublin.

In order to implement his ideas, Rabbi Bunim assembled around him only young *hasidim*, young bridegrooms who ate at their father-in-law's table. One could say that initially this was primarily a youth movement. He studied with an elite group of students who were erudite, had sharp minds and profound understanding, the elite *hasidim* of the Yehudi. They had cast off all the affairs of life, their wives, their children, their relatives, and were totally dedicated to their new leader. They stayed weeks and months in Pshis'cha, engaging themselves in the improvement of hasidism. They used to walk with their rabbi outside of the city in the forests to hear teachings from his lips.

In the courts of the other *tsadikim* of that generation, there were ample provisions and the *hasidim* who came there for Shabbat were given food from the rabbi's house. In Pshis'cha, however, there were very few business-type people to support the young men and the rabbi. They were very needy. People did not come to ask advice and to receive wonders and signs and leave a donation. Rabbi Simcha Bunim did not perform wonders. "Signs and wonders" he used to say, "are in the land of the heathens." They came only to learn Torah and had no money. Therefore, it was very difficult for the rabbi to provide for his *hasidim*. Even the *Shvuim Pidyon* (donors of redemption money given to rescue those in prison) didn't come there. Therefore, the *hasidim* didn't receive anything at all. Hasidism in Pshis'cha was only for truly noble and completely dedicated people.

Performance of the *mitsvot* was most valued, but only if they were without ulterior motives, such as pride, honour, or money. According to the words of Rabbi Bunim, "*Binah*, 'understanding', is light and the deed is secret. Therefore, *binah*, the understanding, is greater than the deed." The essential thing for him was *binah*, understanding. One of the Pshis'cha students, Rabbi Chanoch from Alexander, said, "I am the understanding—when I understand, I have strength... then I am able to stand my ground!"

Rabbi Yitschak Meir Alter, the rabbi of Gur, said, "According to Pshis'cha hasidism, 'Man shouldn't be driven by his physical being, but the essential thing is his inner nature and from there comes the drive for action.'" That is why Pshis'cha *hasidim* spent a lot of time learning from philosophic books of the Middle Ages, *Guide to the Perplexed*, *Kuzari*, and *Mivchar Hapnim* by Rabbi Yedia Hapnini. They also greatly admired the books of the Maharal of

Prague and they devoted much time studying them. Rabbi Simcha Bunim expressed great admiration for the Maharal and said that in the higher world the Maharal was his rabbi. He also favoured the commentaries of Avraham Ibn Ezra on the Torah and noted that one can achieve greatness only by taking *Yir'at HaShamayim* to the highest level. In Polish Judaism in general, and hasidism in particular, engaging in the philosophic books at that time was a great innovation. Pshis'cha *hasidim*, however, were not satisfied with merely philosophic research. They wanted to apply these teachings to their daily lives. They began to disparage the importance of the practical *mitsvot*. For example, at Rosh Hashanah they didn't spend all day praying, as was the custom throughout all the dispersed of Israel. They would get up at dawn and pray all their prayers quickly even to the blowing of the *shofar*, and at the time that most people of the city were going to the synagogue to pray, they were sitting and studying Talmud and *Tosafot* or philosophic books. Their purpose was to accentuate this behaviour, illustrating that their opinions were not in accordance with the customs of the people. They wanted to highlight to the people that they, the people, lacked awareness of the need for preparation of the inner spirit.

These kinds of overt actions aroused the anger of many other *hasidim* and *mitnagdim*. Terror gripped both the hasidic leaders and the *mitnagdim* when they were confronted with this new direction in Pshis'cha. They considered this new movement a danger to tradition and began to scream and rail against it. One of the great opponents of Rabbi Bunim, Rabbi Meir from Apta asked Rabbi Bunim, "Why are your *hasidim* delaying the time of the prayer, as opposed to the time that is set forth in the law of the *Shulchan Aruch*?" He answered him, "As it is written in the prayer, 'man should always know *yir'ah* before G-d, whether hidden or revealed, whether secretly or openly. He should acknowledge truth and speak the truth that is in his heart.'" Thus, he got up at dawn and he said, "Whoever has *Yir'at HaShamayim* in secret or openly, should arise and pray at its time. But those who have not arrived at this level are obligated to prepare themselves in order to reach to an expanded level of consciousness so that they can pray properly."

Pshis'cha *hasidim* especially scorned the populist *tsadikim*, "the wonder workers" and their phoney remedies and their amulets. An Apta *hasid* once received from his rabbi a remedy against his sickness, a white silk belt, to wrap around him at the time of the *Tefillah*. When a Pshis'cha *hasid* saw the belt, he took it and smeared it with pitch. Such was the scorn of Pshis'cha *hasidim*.

One of the fundamental tasks of Pshis'cha hasidism was to uproot the trait of pride and self-glorification. They saw that many truthful and pious people were not completely free from this inclination. They felt that their prayers, their learning and their good deeds were still mixed with a barely detectable small but real sense of superiority. No matter how small that inclination, they felt that it muddied all the purity of the good deed. Consequently, the Pshis'cha *hasidim* tried in every way to uncover and root out these base ulterior motives, in spite of the fact that they were often hidden in many guises and costumes. To achieve this goal, they dispensed judgment equally to all. Rich and poor were confronted, as well as old and young, scholars and the uneducated. They showed no partiality to their friends. They ignored the accepted etiquette of politeness. Woe to the one in whom they saw the inclination for self-glorification. They used to insult him by rebuking and scorning him until he arrived at a level of acknowledging and accepting true values. They used to mock and deride the so-called 'Beautiful Jews', pillars of society. In their eyes, they abolished all the class distinctions that were common at that time in Polish communities.

One can understand how these actions inflamed all the major Jewish leaders and turned them against Pshis'cha *hasidim* and they came to be seen as enemies. Both the other *hasidim* and the *mitnagdim* were totally opposed to them. Rabbi Meir from Apta sent a message to Rabbi Simcha Bunim saying, "How dare he act as a rabbi of *hasidim*! Did he derive these traits in Danzig, and in theatres in Ashkenaz, or in the pharmacy?" Rabbi Bunim responded to his words in this way, "Rabbi Meir does not know how one sins and in what one sins. But I, who was in Danzig and in theatre, know how to heal sinners and how to bring my *hasidim* to revere G-d." The opponents of Pshis'cha felt that, in Pshis'cha, the drive to root out pride and ulterior motives and the striving for *Yir'at HaShamayim* took precedence over the practice of *mitsvot* and that that was the way of heretics.

The Pshis'cha *hasidim* based their behaviour on the writings of Ibn Pakuda, author of *Duties of the Heart*. He wrote,

> *When the evil inclination despairs of enticing you this way, it will try to entice you by suggesting that you avoid all hypocrisy. It will say to you: 'You will be unable to achieve perfection in the wholehearted service of G-d unless you have rid yourself of all forms of currying favour, large and small.' The only way to avoid currying favour with others is by concealing from them your religious activities and by showing them the opposite of what is in your heart...Do not display any good traits. Appear to be lazy and lethargic in serving G-d, so that you do not make a name for yourself*

and lose your reward. Do not urge others to do what is right or warn them against wrong. Do not publicize your knowledge and do not teach it to others. Show no sign of reverence for G-d, nor any evidence of serving Him, so that people not honour you for these virtues.

Duties of the Heart, Vol. II, translated by Daniel Haberman

For the Pshis'cha *hasidim*, an action that stems from a pure heart and knowledge is more important than many deeds that are done without intention and understanding. Every activity that didn't stem from absolute truth was deemed unfit in their eyes. In order to distance themselves from ulterior motives, they used to prefer to do strange activities. Despite all the opposition, the Pshis'cha *hasidim* gathered around their prominent rabbi with love and a deep commitment. Except for some of the *hasidim*, who traveled to the regions around Pshis'cha, there developed a special 'Holy Fellowship' for those who sat and were engaged in Torah and hasidism with Rabbi Simcha Bunim. He used to teach regular daily lessons in Talmud, Rambam, *Midrash* and books of the Maharal.

When tragedy occurred and Rabbi Simcha Bunim became blind, his most distinguished students of the Fellowship would read to him.

These would include some of the great rabbis of Israel such as Rabbi Mendel of Kotsk, Rabbi Yitschak Meir of Gur, Rabbi Chanoch from Alexander, Rabbi Shmuel Sheinaver, and others. They were all leaders in Torah and piety. At the time of the lessons, they paid close attention to the "new insights on the Torah" that were expounded. Anyone who didn't introduce a new insight at the time of the lessons and didn't excel in original ideas was somewhat distanced from the Fellowship.

Of course, Rabbi Simcha Bunim, himself, was opposed to the extreme form that his teachings took among many of his *hasidim*. The fate of his teachings was like the fate of all systems where there is a broad scope and a spiritual vision guided by a charismatic leader. Some people may not be capable or worthy of the system because that which may work for wise and intelligent persons often is inappropriate for limited consciousness of lay people. They may cause even more moral damage. Not all of his *hasidim* understood his ways and some of them were not worthy to be included among his outstanding and distinguished students.

The grumblings against the Pshis'cha movement continued to grow until it encompassed all the *tsadikim* in Galicia and some of the *tsadikim* of Poland. Among the active opponents were Rabbi Naftali from Rovshits, Rabbi Tsvi from Zidtsov, Rabbi Moshe from

Koznits, the son of the Magid, Rabbi Meir from Apta, Rabbi Yosef from Yaritshov, and others. They also attempted to convince the most elder *tsadik*, Rabbi Avraham Joshua Heschel, the Rabbi of Apta, to join them in excommunicating Rabbi Simcha Bunim and all his followers and to separate them from the community of Israel, as had been done previously to the Karaites.

They found the perfect opportunity to do this at the time of a gathering of all the *tsadikim* in the city of Ostila. The renowned wedding of the houses of the *tsadikim* from Naschiz and Radvil was scheduled to take place soon to which all the hasidic leaders and famous spokesmen were invited. At the time of this gathering in Ostila, the opponents of Pshis'cha plotted to raise the issue of the excommunication of the Pshis'cha *hasidim*. They hoped to succeed in influencing the Rabbi from Apta, to give his stamp of approval to their plot.

When Rabbi Simcha Bunim received the invitation to participate in the hasidic celebration in Ostila from the Rabbi of Apta, he wanted to travel there to defend himself against all the charges that had been levelled at him by his opponents. However, his student, R. Menachem Mendel from Kotsk, fearing that his rabbi would not be treated respectfully, would in no way allow him to travel to Ostila. Rabbi Simcha Bunim agreed with his opinion and said to him: "When we are around our table, we are not intimidated by them and do not have to justify ourselves. However, for the sake of peace, we will send representatives to defend us." It was decided to send a special delegation of five of the best of his *hasidim*, who would defend Pshis'cha hasidism. So the Pshis'cha delegation included: a great scholar in Torah, a devout *hasid*, a brilliant rabbi, a wealthy enlightened one, and a formidable orator.

The Torah scholar was Rabbi Yitschak Meir Alter, the Rabbi of Gur, who was known as one of the great scholars of the generation and who wrote the book, *Chidushei HaRim*. The *hasid* was Rabbi Feivel, the rabbi from Geretsa, known for his great piety. The clever one was Rabbi Alexander Zisha, the rabbi from Flotsk, a famous erudite *hasid* and right hand man to Rabbi Simcha Bunim, who wrote down the teachings of his rabbi in the book, *Kol Simcha*. The wealthy one, Rabbi Yissachar Dov Horowitz (the son-in-law of Berko Bergson and Tamar), was also erudite and one of Warsaw's very distinguished and enlightened members of society. Rabbi Eliezer Dov of Grovovits was chosen as the orator, who was known for his eloquence and his speaking ability, often referred to as a 'silver tongued orator'. This delegation made an amazing impression at the Ostila wedding.

About two hundred rabbis and *tsadikim* wrapped in white gathered there from all the hasidic centres in Vohlin, Poland, and Galicia. Indeed, the opponents of Pshis'cha vehemently began their attack against the hasidism of

Pshis'cha in front of the Rabbi of Apta and all those gathered around. They spoke about the scant learning of Torah of the Pshis'cha *hasidim*, their discounting of the practical *mitsvot*, their lack of etiquette, and the negative attitudes displayed toward the rest of the *hasidim* who opposed them. But the great scholar, Rabbi Yitschak of Gur, and the rest of the delegation proved by their appearance and their debate that they had nothing to fear from Pshis'cha.

They said that *hasidim* need not be afraid of negative outcomes coming from Pshis'cha's new direction. Pshis'cha did not intend to found a new sect in Israel. Rather, it merely wanted to inject greater vitality and understanding in hasidism, itself, and it did not in any way intend to stray from the laws of Torah. Rabbi Yerachmiel of Pshis'cha, the son of the Yehudi, testified on behalf of Rabbi Simcha Bunim, relating that his father had said that he had left the treasure of piety with Rabbi Simcha Bunim. His words made a strong impression on the gathering. Finally, the Rabbi of Apta said to Rabbi Shimon Ashkenazi, the head of the opponents, "You are leaders of the dispute and instigators of the quarrel that stemmed from the days of the Seer and the Yehudi. If you were in the forested wilderness, you would quarrel with the trees." With such harsh words, he put an end to their arguments and Pshis'cha hasidism received equal rights among the various streams of hasidism. The delegation returned to Pshis'cha completely vindicated.

Chapter 5

REASONS FOR THE OPPOSITION TO PSHIS'CHA

The private observance of the mitsvot awakened opposition. Public prayer on time. The resemblance to "Chabad". Attitude of the mitnagdim to Pshis'cha. A letter of Rabbi Eliezer Charlap. Rabbi Simcha Bunim's response.

In spite of the victory of the Pshis'cha delegates at the Ostila wedding which saved Pshis'cha *hasidim* from excommunication, the hasidic opposition to the concepts that were being disseminated in Pshis'cha did not abate. They were also joined by the *mitnagdim*. They especially did not agree to go along with Pshis'cha's interpretation of the trait of modesty. "Modesty meant 'to walk humbly with your G-d' (Micah 6:8) and is praiseworthy indeed," said the Pshis'cha *hasidim*. They were concerned that if one were to do *mitsvot* publicly it might lead a person to pride, G-d forbid.

Pshis'cha *hasidim* valued the performance of the *mitsvot* only in so far as they were done with a pure inner intention. The Pshis'cha *hasidim* believed that worshipping G-d had to be completely pure and clean, without any mixture of self-aggrandizement, self-glorification or other

39

self-centered biases. If the *mitsvot* were performed in a mechanical external manner, without the holy spark, then their value was considered null and void.

The Pshis'cha *hasidim's* behaviour of delaying the time of prayer and not praying publicly until they were ready to pray with the intention of a completely focused consciousness stirred up enormous anger. The great hasidic and mitnagdic leaders strongly opposed this idea. In their opinion, a Jew needs to practice the *mitsvot* literally, according to the laws of the *Shulchan Aruch*, and if they are done with intention and purity, all the better, but if the intention is lacking, it does not prevent one from performing the *mitsvot* openly. Rabbi Meir of Apta wrote:

> *There is a major principle in the worship of HaShem. One, who has not completed his observance, should not look too deeply. Initially he need only do his best to fix his practical observance. There is no need to act beyond a person's strength, but only with the abilities with which G-d has graced him. The vessels were broken because they couldn't stand the radiance of the Divine light. A person should not seek after more understanding than that which exceeds his ability, even if his intention is 'for the sake of G-d'. The essence of the correct path*

is to walk gradually according to one's own capability. It is forbidden for humans to attempt to probe great wisdoms and counsels. Rather, the human who wants to return to 'The Blessed One' needs to work on repairing his character traits to the maximum. Perhaps afterwards he may manage to achieve an integrity which is the secret of 'knowing' G-d.

Rabbi Naftali Tsvi from Rofshits wrote, "The ways of Moshe and Aaron were not to choose except what G-d chose and not to go beyond themselves and aspire higher than that which is more wondrous than their own understanding."

One of the *mitnagdim* wrote,

There is a simple path in the worship of G-d to do all the mitsvot truthfully, to publicly pray and on time, to distance one's self from all kinds of fun and idle ramblings. This is called the path of the righteous! There is still another path: that is to say, some times not to pray publicly, and at times to delay the time of the Tefilah, so that one should not pray with superfluous intention and like matters. This is how wicked people act, saying it is for the sake of Torah.

41

Rabbi Kolonymos from Cracow wrote,

About the terms of the worship service, a person should not deviate one step, even a hair's breadth. To transgress the warning of the Torah, the warning of the Talmud and the latter sages who said that, it is as if everyone who withdraws from their words, withdraws from life. These people, thinking that their prayer is more exalted, allow themselves to forego the words of the poskim and no longer pray their prayer at the prescribed time. The worship of these people will be in vain and futile. A person who approaches the worship service should examine all this, so that he does not aim his prayer in the direction of wondrous and concealed things that G-d has hidden. You will not find the ways of Torah in one who pretends to elevate himself while his thoughts wander about the Divine. His deeds are not desirable.

Rabbi Naftali Tsvi from Rofshits quotes,

'I implore G-d at that time.'(Deut. 3:23). 'At that time,' he did not say at which time in order to teach us that a person should not say: "At this time I do not have the proper

consciousness for the prayer so I will not pray at this time"—or he might say, "I will pray properly and correctly only if I feel open to it." But rather he should pray at the actual prescribed time whenever that time presently is

As a result of such behaviour, the following significant *tsadikim* were also against them: Rabbi Baruch from Mizboz, Rabbi Mordechai from Lichobits, Rabbi Avraham from Kalisk, to Rabbi Shneur Zalman from Liadi, the profound scholar in hasidism who was elevated to the level of a Talmudic philosopher. They said, "*HaBakuk* formulated it all in one principle, i.e. a *tsadik* will live by his faith, a pure and simple faith." But Rabbi Shneur Zalman of Liadi said, "Just as it is impossible for a man to beget children without a mother, so it is impossible to be pious without contemplation."

Both the *hasidim* and the *mitnagdim* were against R. Simcha Bunim. We have a manuscript of a letter that was written to Rabbi Simcha Bunim from the very scholarly Rabbi Tsvi Eliezer Charlap, head of the Court of Tiktin. In this letter, he listed every Pshis'cha sin. He expressed his utter abhorrence against some of the Pshis'cha *hasidim*, who transgress the laws of the *Shulchan Aruch*, and wrote that he "…sends sharp arrows to them for despising the sages, because all the sages of the Gemara are like nothing to them… On the 17th of Tammuz, in broad daylight, they ate, and during the mourning of Tisha B'Av they rejoiced, turning it into a celebration!"

He asked Rabbi Bunim to make every effort to influence his *hasidim* to mend their ways. "It is within his (Simcha Bunim's) power. G-d has his hand," wrote Rabbi Charlap "and he, Rabbi Simcha Bunim, has the ability to save our holy Torah." Indeed, Rabbi Charlap urged Rabbi Simcha Bunim "with his whole heart and soul that you do this." The rabbi requested that Rabbi Simcha Bunim use his influence with his *hasidim* "to submit to the Talmudic sages so that they will be nurtured by the breasts of the Torah experience. They should follow the debates of Abaya and Rava and not deviate neither to the right nor to the left from the traditional laws of our sages and from the *Shulchan Aruch* that is set before us." He writes, "We are gripped with terror. It is not enough that they do not treat each other respectfully. The lesser despises the greater. They also consider slandering a great *mitsvah*."

Finally, he addressed Rabbi Bunim, saying,

> *For the sake of His holy name, May He be Blessed, and our holy Torah, I pray that you will heed my words. You should accept the positive intention of this letter and not accept the negativity because I wrote from extreme anger at the*

insult to the Torah and its students. I'm not condemning you and your followers who bring such disgrace and shame, but rather condemning those who distort the words of Torah. I know this would not occur to you nor to the least learned among our people, who really uphold our holy Torah.

The letter focused on the great value of learning Torah and performing the *mitsvot* and was sprinkled with the words of the Talmudic sages, and the *Zohar*. This letter was written in "fiery words in a fiery speech". It made a great impression in Pshis'cha.

This is the answering letter that was written to the aforementioned Rav:

17th day of Mar Cheshvan in the year___

Greetings and Blessings, the scholarly rabbi and our teacher, Eliezer Tsvi Hirsh Charlap, may his light shine, Head of the Court of Atsutsin:

I hear his strong and fiery voice walking between fiery stones, and understand that "open reproof is better than concealed love" and "faithful are the wounds of a friend" of G-d and the Holy Torah (Proverbs 27:5,6). "Let the righteous man strike me" (Psalm 141:5) with disgrace and so much more. I know that he speaks not from jealousy and hatred, but rather from the fiery zeal for G-d that is within him and from the like-minded flame of the love of G-d. I have heard about his wisdom, his piety and his great learning and the honoured veritable treasure both revealed and hidden from the mouth of our teacher, our rabbi, Rabbi Yitschak from Lublin, may his memory be for a blessing, and also the great scholar, Yitschak, the Yehudi, may his memory be for a blessing, who never deviated from loving him, and whose praise was always on his lips. Thus my spirit complies with his commands and perhaps I will be able to do so. I have done much and will continue to do so for the sake of His Holy Name, may He be blessed, and His love be in my heart "And all sins be covered with love"(Proverbs 10:12) Peace to Your Honour and his teachings.

Sincerely,

These are the words of Rabbi Simcha Bunim, the son of our teacher, Rabbi Tvi Hirsh, may his memory be for a blessing.

According to different sources, Rabbi

Simcha Bunim did his best to convince his *hasidim* not to transgress, nor overdo its measure. He urged then not to extract from his teachings such conclusions that are in contradiction with the accepted tradition and customs and practices.

Chapter 6

THE ATTITUDE OF PSHIS'CHA TOWARD THE POLITICAL LIFE OF POLISH JEWS

The Duchy of Warsaw. The hopes of Jews for equal rights. Russian politics relating to Jews. The Poles and the Jews. Regulations about the Assembly of the People of the Old Testament, also known as the Adherents of the Old Testament. Rabbi Simcha Bunim as a member of the Assembly. Decrees on hasidism. The debate.

Napoleon and his army marched eastward. Polish blood flowed like water. The victories of Napoleon, the conqueror of nations, brought hope to the country that had been partitioned by Prussia, Austria, and Russia. In exchange for their assistance, the Polish people hoped to benefit from this war and that their country would be restored. Napoleon installed Frederick Augustus from Saxony, the grandson of the last king of Poland, as king. Napoleon subsequently established the Duchy of Warsaw, which contained ten regions that were taken from the former partitioners of Poland. For a short time, 1807-1812, Poland rose to prominence. With the renewed Polish kingdom, the Jews too hoped for an improvement in their situation, including the granting of equal rights. They especially felt that they deserved this right, after exhibiting their loyalty to Poland at the time of the siege of Praga, the twin city of Warsaw. Six hundred Jews fell there, slain in the defence of the capital city under the command of General Barak Yoselovits.

A spirit of freedom and liberty prevailed in all the countries that were conquered by Napoleon. Polish Jews, especially the *maskilim*, were certain that a golden era of equal rights would ensue for them as well. However, in the following years, Napoleon issued the shameful "religion edict" of 1808, in which he cancelled for ten years the equal rights of the Jews throughout his jurisdiction. The Poles were very pleased with this law. They immediately published an edict stating that, "residents of the Warsaw Duchy who observe the Mosaic Religion are prevented the usage of Polish rights for ten years." The Poles hoped that within this time the Jews would get rid of the special characteristics that differentiated them so much from their neighbours in the land.

From that day on, the list of increased restrictions in the lives of Polish Jews began. They were forbidden to buy any of the inherited lands of the aristocracy and their rights to reside in Warsaw were also severely restricted. In the year 1812, an edict was issued prohibiting Jews from trading in whiskey or owning any taverns for the following two years. The sole purpose of this decree was to deprive tens of thousands of families from their major livelihood. This situation lasted until 1813. With the defeat of Napoleon, the "Duchy of Warsaw" ended.

Alexander the First, Tsar of Russia, became King of Poland and the Polish state became subordinate to Russia. The autonomy that had been promised to the Polish people at the Congress in Vienna in 1815 was very limited. With the changing of the guard, there also came a change in the attitudes toward Jews. The new deputy for the Russian government in Poland, the Governor Novosiltsov, saw himself as a "lover of Israel." He drew representatives of the Jews closer to him and behaved sympathetically toward them, attempting to soften the previous evil decree. From time to time he even put changes in the orders of the Russian king, the pious one, for the benefit of the Jews. His motivation was not out of piety or for the well-being of Jews, but rather to harm the Poles. This politician wanted to sow hatred between Poles and Jews. He attempted to sway the Jewish residents in favour of the Russians. He wanted to convince them that they could receive rights and humane treatment only from the Russian government and not from the Poles. With the rise of Russian rule and based on the advice of Novosiltsov, a Jewish delegation from the Warsaw Assembly immediately went and stood before the Tsar, Alexander I, in Paris and also in St. Petersburg, in 1815. They requested the cancellation of the order that forbade Jews to engage in the sale of brandy and in distilleries. The Tsar granted them their request and the implementation of the previous order was rescinded. The Jews of Poland greatly rejoiced upon the cancellation of the evil decree, which would have brought economic disaster upon them. Consequently, they were grateful to the Tsar, Alexander, their defender and saviour from the hands of the Poles.

With the renewed autonomy of communities, Novosiltsov, himself, also proposed to give equal rights to Polish Jews and to improve their way of life based on the model of European culture.

However, the Poles were militantly opposed to this suggestion. They portrayed the Jews in these words:

> *The Jews keep to themselves as though in a state, like a foreign nation. Their increase in population in the realm of Poland is terrifying. In the year 1790, their numbers were 1/13 of all the inhabitants, and presently they are 1/8 of the population. By marrying while still young, they are fruitful and multiply immeasurably. They don't get drunk. They are tricksters, content with little. They become wealthy by swindling or deceit. Shirkers of hard work, they don't*

*create anything. Rather they live off
the avails of workers and impoverish
them. If we do not set the rules in
order to take advantage of the useful
traits of the Jews for the good of the
general public, they will eventually
succeed in destroying all the sources
of wealth of the people, because they
are liable to rise above Christians
and bring them to the point of
despair.*

These were the images of Jews held by the Poles.
Thus it was clearly understood that in this
environment, there was no possible way to
conceive of equal rights for Jews.

The espoused goal of the kingdom of
Poland was the spiritual assimilation of the Jews.
Poles believed that only then would Polish Jewry
be sufficiently prepared to receive equal rights. It
was the opinion of the aristocracy of Poland that
first, one would need to "correct" the
mannerisms, characteristics, and attributes of the
masses of Jews. They started the reform process
by forbidding them to trade in wine and spirits.
That would impoverish them and thereby bring
them closer to tilling the soil and turn them into
peasants like other Poles. The Poles also intended
to eliminate the self-rule of the community and
transform their religious educational system into
a civil secular system. They wished to follow the
model of Western Europe, which succeeded in
assimilating the Jews among their nations in a

relatively short period of time. Western European Jewry seemed to reject what appeared to Poles as all the ignorant customs and worthless opinions practiced among Polish Jews.

In order to advance this goal of assimilation, in the year 1825, the government established a special committee on Jewish affairs in Warsaw. It was called "the Committee of the People of the Old Testament". Members of the committee were Polish officers. However, alongside the committee, a Jewish Council was formed with representatives from the capital city and from rural towns. The representatives from the Warsaw community were the following: representing the *mitnagdim* were Michael Ettinger, Yitschak Yonah, and the scholar, Rabbi Shlomo Pozner; representing the *maskilim* were Avraham Shtern, the mathematician and father-in-law of N. H. Z. Slonimski; and representing the *hasidim* were Yaacov Zonenberg-Bergson, the son of Tamar Bergson, and others. From the rural towns, came a few respected merchants and also Rav Shlomo Ashkenaz, the head of the court in Lublin. Rabbi Simcha Bunim from Pshis'cha was also a representative from the district of Tsuzmir. He was liked by the ruling powers because of his erudition in knowing several languages and his modernity in everyday matters, as well as the fact that he represented *hasidim*.

At the beginning of the establishment of the committee, the Jews held high hopes of obtaining equal rights and an economic improvement of their situation. However, its true face was quickly revealed as the evil intentions of the government of Poland became known to all. The Polish 'scholar' Kyarini, a professor of Middle Eastern studies at the University of Warsaw and an enemy of Judaism, was invited to the committee in his capacity as an 'expert on Jewish affairs.' This 'expert' boasted about his great knowledge of Talmud which he drew from Eisenmenger's book, *Judaism Uncovered*.

In Kyarini's own book, *The Teachings of Judaism*, Kyarini claimed that he could actually prove the reality of the famous "blood libel" claim and other similar lies and falsehoods. Noted scholars like Togenhold in Warsaw, and Yost and Tsonts in Germany, had already laid bare his ignorance in matters of Judaism and Talmud and they came out strongly against his teachings. The policies of the committee caused great disappointment in Jewish circles in Poland. The preliminary work of the committee resulted in the following five decisions:

1) The founding of an academy for rabbis.

2) The founding of Jewish folk schools in which "they will prepare Jewish youth to recognize the false teaching of Talmud". With the founding of these schools, the *chadarim* and *yeshivot* will be closed.

3) Censorship of Hebrew books.

4) The translation of the Babylonian Talmud for the use of those engaged in the reforming of Judaism.

5) The training of Christian officials in Hebrew and Talmud so that they can implement all the changes needed in Judaism.

Kyarini was selected as teacher in this academy.

It is easy to understand the feelings that these decisions aroused among Polish Jewry. The overwhelming majority of Polish Jewry were *mitnagdim* and *hasidim* who were faithful to traditional Judaism. Even the moderate *maskilim* were opposed to these changes. When the government offered the position of principal of this so-called rabbinic academy to the scholar, Avraham Shtern, he refused to accept the position. He reasoned that the academy would only bring moral corruption and the destruction of Judaism because religious studies received a trivial place in the curriculum and the faculty was not qualified for its task. The position of principal was ultimately given to the extreme assimilationist, Antony Eisenboim. The teacher of Hebrew and Bible was Avraham Bochner, who published slander against the Talmud, and helped Kyarini, the enemy of Judaism, in his so-called scientific literary work on the Talmud.

Rabbi Simcha Bunim from Pshis'cha, of course, together with all of Polish Jewry, was strongly opposed to the activities of the Committee of the People of the Old Testament.

His student, Rabbi Yitschak from Vorkah, proposed "a public fast" by all the Jews of Poland as a symbol of their determination to abolish the committee and its regulations. Polish Jews declared a holy war against the reform and assimilationist agenda of the government. The controversy surrounding the regulations of the committee continued for several years. Novosiltsov, the Russian governor, was in Warsaw at the time. He intervened 'on behalf' of those concerned. Rabbi Simcha Bunim from Pshis'cha persisted in his activities against the committee till the year of his death in 1827. His aforementioned students continued his work until three years later when the revolt against Russian rule broke out. The government of Poland changed and all these plans came to an end.

While defending the hasidic movement, Rabbi Simcha Bunim had the opportunity to express his views about the authority of the "Committee of the People of the Old Testament" and about the government laws relating to the Jews. It happened that the Committee of the District of Plotsk wished to demonstrate to the central government powers that they were true to their mandate of implementing measures which would further the assimilation of its Jews. Therefore, it banned prayer in the private houses, *shtibelach* of the hasidim, citing the following rationale: "in order to uproot superstition and delusions... and in order that Jews will be completely elevated to a level of our civilization by gradual degrees of enlightenment so that they will become useful to the state and resemble the rest of the inhabitants." Thus the Committee justified its right to issue this decree.

In a special memorandum, the government requested that the Jewish community of Warsaw clarify the essence of hasidism and answer whether hasidism brings damage to the Israelite religion or enlightenment to the masses. Yaacov Zonenberg-Bergson, the son of Tamar and an admirer of hasidism, was at that time head of the Jewish community in Warsaw. He responded that according to their completed investigation, the *hasidim* were not at all different from the rest of the followers of the Mosaic religion, other than that they prayed in special hasidic houses and that they could be distinguished by their extra fervour in prayer, and also that they sang enthusiastically during prayer time. He wrote that such movements existed even before the current emergence of hasidism.

In their desire to do a more thorough investigation, the government sent one of her high officials to question both Rabbi Meir of Apta and Rabbi Simcha Bunim of Pshis'cha. Rabbi Meir represented the popular stream of hasidism and Rabbi Bunim represented a scholarly elite. When the official asked Rabbi Meir of Apta why he prayed with such fervour, he responded, "My heart within me is warm and like fire it burns throughout my meditations." Rabbi Simcha Bunim's erudition in the languages of German, Polish and Italian, his wisdom and his European clothing and manners made a great impression on the official. Rabbi Bunim said to the official, "It is not the task of the state to interfere in the internal affairs of the Jews. The government should leave these questions for the rabbis and the *tsadikim*. The duty of the government toward the Jews is to look into their material conditions and to try to reduce the poverty that is so widespread among Polish Jewry." These words made a great impression upon the few *maskilim* who appeared there at the time. They felt warmly to the only rabbi who was so distinguished with a general education and broad life experience. The result of these government visits and investigations was the issuing of a law in the year 1823, in which it was permissible for *hasidim* to pray in hasidic houses and the giving of complete freedom to hasidic movements.

Chapter 7

HIS LATTER YEARS AND HIS DEATH

His ethical influence. The words of the students around him. The attitudes of the maskilim. His spiritual greatness. His death. His successors and his students.

In Simcha Bunim's latter years, his teachings reached their peak. Thousands, from all walks of life, came to Pshis'cha to hear his hasidic teachings. He was honoured and admired even in the circles of the *maskilim* and *mitnagdim*, as they saw in this rabbi one who understood the spirit of the times. Rabbi Simcha Bunim taught Torah from the perspective of intellectual enlightenment and analytic research.

In spite of the fact that he became blind in his latter days, "the magic of grace inundated his lips". His spoken words of wisdom and intelligence always made a great impression on his listeners. He accepted his suffering with serenity and love: "I, Bunim," he once said according to his *hasidim*, "prayed to the Master of the Universe, who cast out the light of my eyes, in order that my eyes will be open to see a deeper everlastingness and the radiance of eternity." His ethical influence was very great as his closest students saw in it "a Divine component that is impossible to explain intellectually." "Everyone who saw his face," his *hasidim* said, "never left without repenting."

One of the *mitnagdim* of Pshis'cha, Rabbi Yishai of Pshedborz, once asked Rabbi Yitschak of Vorka, "What is the reason for your admiration of Rabbi Simcha Bunim? What is his great secret?" Rabbi Yitschak replied, "When the prophet Elijah met Elisha, 'he came upon Elisha...while he was ploughing with twelve pair of oxen...so Elijah went over to him and cast his mantle upon him'." (Kings Chapt.19 v.19). Rabbi Yitschak explained further, saying,

> *Elisha was a simple farmer, but when Elijah threw his mantle upon him, he immediately left the oxen and ran after Elijah, and said, "Please let me kiss my father and mother goodbye, and then I will follow you." Elijah asked him, "What have I done to you?" This is the secret of prophetic influence. When Rabbi Simcha Bunim touched our hands and spoke to us his words of Torah, we were immediately enthusiastic and filled with a closeness to G-d and a love of G-d and we became purified like Elisha in his time.*

The scholar, Rabbi Meir Yitschak Alter of Gur said: "up until the happening of Pshis'cha, hasidism was interpreting the Besht. But from the time of Pshis'cha, hasidism was interpreting

Pshis'cha."

Although the *haskalah* was waging a holy war against its arch enemy, i.e. hasidism, the *maskilim* and assimilationist circles felt a great love and admiration for Rabbi Simcha Bunim. Yitschak Mezas from Galicia came from the followers of such noted *maskilim* as Rabbi Nachman Krochmal and Rabbi Solomon Judah Leib Rapoport, otherwise known by his acronym "the Shir".

In the days of his youth, Yitschak Mezas traveled to Pshis'cha and became one of Rabbi Bunim's students. He liked to boast that Rabbi Simcha Bunim honoured and favoured him by inviting him to lead *Birkat HaMazon*. In turn, Mezas returned a similar devotion to R. Bunim. Nevertheless, after the death of Rabbi Simcha Bunim, Yitschak Mezas became an ardent *maskil*, founding the first *maskil* synagogue in Krakow, and authoring books in German on Jewish thought. His most famous book written in German, *Deciphering the Hidden*, dealt with the essence of *Kabalah*. Mezas said that there was no resemblance between the wisdom of Rabbi Simcha Bunim and the presumed teachings of Rabbi Bunim that were subsequently published in *Kol Simcha (The Voice of Simcha)*. According to Rabbi Yitschak's words, Rabbi Bunim was "...a philosophizing and investigating person who knew German, Polish, and Italian. He was a pharmacist who recruited his soldiers from his most distinguished Torah students, the finest

61

gold. He attracted to him all the youth who were both knowledgeable in Torah and highly spiritual." According to Yitschak Mezas, Rabbi Simcha Bunim was one of the great spiritual leaders of his time in all of Europe.

Rabbi Shmuel Sheinover, was head of the court of many communities in Poland, wrote the book, *Ramatayim Tsofim (Scouts of the High Places)* which commented on the *Tanna D'Bei Eliyahu (Teachings of the House of Elijah)*, a collection of *midrash*. It is one of the most important and reliable sources of the history and essence of hasidism in Poland. Rabbi Shmuel Sheinover became one of Simcha Bunim's most distinguished students and wrote many words of admiration about him:

> *Rabbi Simcha Bunim never spoke an empty word, Heaven Forbid, and his holy mouth never uttered empty worthless words. I can attest that he never laughed. Even when he was telling us a funny story, he did not laugh. His eyes didn't see and his ears didn't hear worthless or negative speech. Serious thoughts were always seen on his face. He was critical of his young hasidim when their attitudes toward the so-called 'Beautiful Jews' were dismissive or when they didn't behave politely to the elderly and he complained that his hasidim*

> *attributed to him things to which he*
> *was actually opposed.*

Rabbi Simcha Bunim would sit regularly, every day, studying *Gemara* and *Tosefot* with his students. He was known to have had a very sharp mind regarding Talmud, even before he ever became a rabbi. In the learning centre in Pshis'cha, one could find all of Rambam together with many notes. Because he was blind, a select number of students read the lessons to him, not only from the Talmud, but also from the books of the Maharal of Prague, the *Tanna D'Bei Eliyahu (Teachings of the House of Elijah)*, and other research books. As was the custom among Polish Jews, he would study whole sections. He used to solicit from his students that they find new insights in every lesson and every biblical argument. His new insights on different tractates were published in the book, *Kol Simcha (Voice of Simcha)*.

His days of leadership were short, only thirteen years, from 1814 to 1827. However, in those few years, Rabbi Bunim contributed much to the education and vitality of Polish Judaism. Pshis'cha hasidism and those who replaced it— Kotsk, Vorkah, and Gur—excelled in a love of Torah, of learning, original thinking, and an alertness to Jewish issues. Polish hasidism kept its freshness and lasted a long time, more so than in other countries. Rabbi Bunim attracted many *hasidim* and the results of his obvious influence still last today.

Rabbi Shmuel Sheinover related that upon his approaching death, Rabbi Simcha Bunim saw his wife, Rivka, crying, and said to her: "Why are you crying? Haven't I devoted all my life so that I would know how to die?" Rabbi Simcha Bunim died on the 12th day in the month of Elul, in the year 1827. He was approximately sixty-five years old. A mausoleum was built on his grave site next to the grave of his mentor, the Yehudi HaKadosh.

In spite of its great decline, Pshis'cha hasidism lives on in the profound influence Rabbi Bunim had upon his followers. After his passing, a split occurred among his *hasidim*. A part of them continued to travel to Pshis'cha, to his son, Rabbi Avraham Moshe, including Rabbi Yitschak and one of his great admirers from Vorka. However, the majority of his followers accepted the authority of Rabbi Menachem Mendel of Kotsk, who was his most outstanding student and who refined Pshis'cha hasidism, bringing it to its highest level, but also to a certain degree of extremism.

The Kotsker *hasidim* mocked the son of Rabbi Simcha Bunim saying, "In Pshis'cha, there remains brandy, a wagon harnessed to four horses, the son of a *tsadik*, and a livelihood." Thus they expressed their opposition to the simple hasidism that was led by Rabbi Avraham Moshe in Pshis'cha. In Kotsk, they didn't think about brandy or livelihood, but rather focused only on spiritual and ethical exaltation.

Although there are no known Pshis'cha *hasidim* today, Rabbi Simcha Bunim's influence extended far beyond his immediate circle. Beside the aforementioned successors, the following notable rabbis and *tsadikim* were among his Pshis'cha *hasidim*: Rabbi Yitschak of Vorka, mentioned many times in our story; Rabbi Shmuel Sheinover, the rabbi in Volodvi and Nishlosk, and author of the book, *Ramatayim Tsofim (Scouts of the High Places)*; Rabbi Yechezkel of Kuzmir, author of *Nechmad Mizahav (More Desirable than Gold)*, and the head of the dynasty of Modzits, known for its splendid musicians and composers of *nigunim*; Rabbi Yaacov of Radzimin, a wonder maker; Rabbi Mordechai Yosef of Izbitsa, author of *Mei Hashiloach (Waters of Shiloah)*, and the sparring partner of Rabbi Mendel of Kotsk, head of the dynasty of Radzin; the grandfather of Rabbi Gershon Chanoch Leiner, the famous scholar and discoverer of the snail that provided the *tchelet* (blue color) for *tsitsit*, and author of *Sidrae Taharot (Orders of Purity)*; R. Yitschak Meir Alter—the first rabbi of Gur, author of *Chidushei Ha'Rym, (Insights of R. Yitschak Meir)*, a scholar and righteous person who succeeded the rabbi of Kotsk; Rabbi Alexander Zisha, head of the court of Flotsk, the author of the book, *Yakar Mipaz (Dearer than Gold)*; and *Kol Simcha (Voice of Simcha)*, supposedly from the lips of Rabbi Simcha Bunim; Rabbi Avraham of Tshechnov, famous scholar and author of many books of Torah insights; Rabbi Chanoch Hinich of Alexander, the successor of Rabbi Yizchak Meir of Gur; Rabbi Shalom Tsvi, the rabbi in Zgiraz; Rabbi Meir Yechiel of Mogilnitsah, a famous *tsadik* and grandson of the preacher of Kovnits; Rabbi Chaim, head of the court of Kalshin and author of *She'eylot V'Tshuvot Pri Chayyim (Questions and Responsa of the Fruit of Life)*; Rabbi Meir Simcha, head of the court in Gomvin, author of *Remzei Aysh (Hints of Fire)*; Rabbi Yaacov Aharon, head of the court in Alexander, author of *Bayt Yaacov (House of Jacob)*; Rabbi Elazar, head of the court in Sochitshov, son-in-law of Rabbi Yaacov of Lisa, and author of the book *Chidushei Maharach (Insights of the Maharach)*; Rabbi Shraga Fievel, head of the court in Gritsa, father of the rabbi of Alexander, and others.

Chapter 8

PSHIS'CHA HASIDISM

Hasidic attitudes to Napoleon. Enlightenment and assimilation. Hasidism and enlightenment. The revival of Sephardic philosophy. The Maharal of Prague. Rabbi Yedayah Hapnini. Chabad and Pshis'cha. The search for truth—a Pshis'cha principle.

In Europe, the spirit of a new awakening was in the air. It seemed as if the European revival had not yet reached Poland. One might think that the ideas of the French Revolution did not impact on any of the extremely ultra-orthodox Jews in Poland at that time, as the vast majority of these Jews belonged to the hasidic movement and were frozen in the practices of earlier times. However, in actual fact, the Napoleonic wars awakened a messianic longing in the hearts of the *tsadikim* of Poland: Rabbi Mendel of Rymanov saw in the conqueror of nations, the steps of the redeemer, who would also bring about the redemption of Israel. At first, the Magid of Koznits thought so too, but in the end, he realized that deliverance did not spring forth from Napoleon. "You shall surely fall," uttered the Magid of Kovnits, "Napoleon will fall!"

The *hasidim* of Poland especially feared the spirit of liberation and freedom that was promised by the French Revolution because they felt it would cause an increase in heresy among Jews. "They showed me," wrote Rabbi Shneur Zalman of Liadi, "that if Bonaparte would be victorious in Anaparta, the wealth of Israel will multiply and the glory of Israel will expand, but the heart of Israel will separate and distance itself from their Father in Heaven. If, however, our Lord Alexander will be victorious, even though the poverty of Israel will increase and the glory of Israel will be diminished, the heart of Israel will be drawn closer and more attached and will bond to their Father in Heaven." Although *hasidim* tried to distance themselves from the influence of France, they did not succeed. There were enticing rumours about the establishment of a Sanhedrin and equal rights for Jews, in the lands that were under the influence of Napoleon.

The *haskalah* movement, led by the students of Moses Mendelson and his followers, was getting ever stronger in Germany and they also had a significant impact in Italy. Until the year 1807, the land of Poland had been under the yoke of those who had partitioned it: Russia, Prussia and Austria. The parts of the interior of Poland, such as Warsaw and Krakow, were under Prussian and Austrian rule. The Jews who lived there were influenced to a great degree by the German based *haskalah* movement. In Warsaw, a new type of Jew was seen who wore

European clothes and gave their children a modern education. These *maskilim*, "attempted to uproot the customs and so-called negative traits that differentiated them from the rest of the local people." Therefore, they were called 'Germans'. The *haskalah* movement grew stronger, especially after 1807, when Napoleon established the principality of Warsaw, which he had appropriated from the regions of Prussia and Austria.

The Principality of Warsaw came under the influence of the ideas of the French Revolution. New winds also began to blow among the nobles of Poland. The majority of writers and Polish statesmen who were dealing with the Jewish problem responded positively to the demands of the Jews and advocated equal rights for them. Jews of the *haskalah*, such as Yaakov Tagenhoff and others, also took part in the debate that had arisen in Polish literature. For the first time, the Jewish scholar, Avraham Shtern, who had published a scientific work in mathematics, appeared among distinguished Polish scientists. He became a member of the Association of Scientists in Poland.

The assimilationist movement that was established in Warsaw was headed by Antony Eisenboim who produced the first Polish-Jewish newspaper, *Hatsofeh al Havistula (The Scout on the Vistula)*. The establishment of the Committee on Jewish Affairs and its demands for reform in the area of Jewish education and, to a large extent, the opening of a *Bet HaMidrash* (House of Study) for rabbis in Warsaw, contributed to the spread of the *haskalah* and its new ideas among the Jews of the Polish interior.

The conflict between hasidism and the *haskalah* is well-known. *Hasidim* fought the *haskalah* movement with all the means at its disposal: by excommunication, persecution, and writings. Similarly, the *maskilim* also saw hasidism as its enemy and directed all its arrows against it, creating a complete literature whose goal was to foster hatred of hasidism in the eyes of the masses.

Some of the *haskalah* leaders in Eastern Galicia who emerged vigorously opposed to hasidism, were: Rabbi Nachman Krochmal, author of *Moreh N'vuchei Hazman (Guide to the Perplexed of the Times)*; Yosef Perel, author of *Migilah Timirim (The Revealer of the Mysterious)* and *Even Bohen (Criteria)*; Yitschak Arter, author of *Tsofeh L'Bet Yisrael (Scout of the House of Israel)*; Rabbi Shlomo Yehudah Leib Rapoport, known as the Shir, author of *Ner Mitsvah (The Light of the Commandment(s))*; I. L. Mezees, author of *T'kanot Harabanim (Virtues of the Rabbis)*; *Kanah Ha-emet (Jealous of the Truth)*, and others. The Russian *maskilim* also joined them, notably the Ryvel and others.

This war between hasidism and the *haskalah* became so bitter that the *haskalah* even denounced the *hasidim* to the authorities: the writer, Rabbi Yosef Perel, denounced Rabbi

Naftali Tsvi of Rofshits and Rabbi Tsvi Eichenshtein. The only one of the group who defended hasidism for national and religious reasons was Rabbi Yaacov Shmuel Bayk, who rebuked Rabbi Shlomo Rapoport and Perel about their negative attitudes toward hasidism. On the other hand, in order to prevent the expansion of the *haskalah* in the interior regions of Poland, the followers of populist hasidism fought an all out war, without giving any concessions to the *maskilim*. The populist hasidic founders, Rabbi Elimelech of Lizensk, the Magid of Kovnits, and the Seer of Lublin, proceeded along the tried and true path of the continuation of learning Torah and applying Besht-type hasidism.

Rabbi Simcha Bunim of Pshis'cha differed from that of the other *tsadikim* of Poland in that he had a special way and focused in a new direction. He attempted to disarm the *maskilim* by using their own weapons. He hoped to establish a new spiritual movement based on substituting Jewish enlightenment for that of gentile culture.

Rabbi Simcha Bunim felt that he was capable of overcoming the *haskalah* movement and that he could fill the thirsty void of secular assimilation offered by the *haskalah*. For this reason, Rabbi Simcha Bunim demanded that his *hasidim* return to the study of Torah, with an expanded and deeper understanding of its words, and return to earlier sources such as Bible, Talmud, the writings of the Middle Ages, theology, Sephardic exegesis, and the books of the Maharal of Prague.

Populist hasidism was essentially nourished by the book, the *Zohar*, and the *Kabalah* of the Ari. Despite their admiration for Rambam, the *hasidim* did not study his works. All the hasidic literature drew from the writings of the Ari, Rabbi Yitschak Luria. Their engagement in *Kabalah* was done rather superficially and was not thoroughly researched. Rabbi Shneur Zalman of Liadi, for example, was very engaged in establishing the ideological foundation of the concepts of *Kabalah* on the Deity. He wrote about the *sephirot* and *tsimtsum* in his books, *Likutei Amarim (Collection of Essays)* and *Sh'ar Hayichud Ha-emunah (A Gate of Unity and Faith)*, and others.

In contrast, the Magid of Koznits, whom everyone agrees was a brilliant and profound scholar in Bible and *Kabalah*, did not engage deeply in abstract matters and wrote little about matters of *tsimtsum*. Instead, he said that "the investigation of that matter is too obtuse for us to attain." Rabbi Simcha Bunim, therefore, was very opposed to this kind of mechanical and superficial learning of *Kabalah*: "There is no one in this generation" he said, "who knows *Kabalah* because in its study one needs to attain the lights."

The *Kabalah* does not occupy considerable space in the book, *Kol Simcha*. There was very little teaching about *tsimtsum*, about the rising of Divine Sparks or the sweetening of the laws, which occupied a lot of space in most of the other hasidic literature at that time. Rabbi Bunim once said to one of his closest *hasidim* that one should ask a master of *Kabalah*, about the secret that is hinted at in the enlarged letter *"Ayin"* in the word *"Shema"* and also in the enlarged letter *"Dalet"* in the word *"echad"*, the last word in the recitation of the *Shema*. According to the law, one can fulfill the obligation of saying the *Shema* in any language, and in the other languages, there is no large *"ayin"* and *"dalet"*. So what happens to the kabbalistic intentions or secret meanings in that case?"

Instead of *Kabalah*, Rabbi Simcha Bunim placed the investigatory writings of the middle ages at the center of his teachings: Rambam, Rabbi Sadia Gaon, and Rabbi Yehudah Halevi. He gave great importance to the study of the books of the Rambam on *halacha* and expressed his wish to publish *Hayad HaChazakah (With a Strong Hand)*, with the references and a short interpretation, so that the numbers of its students and buyers would grow. One *hasid*, Rabbi Yitschak Asher Kihan, actually made it happen. He published parts of the Rambam in a popular edition with a brief interpretation.

Rabbi Simcha Bunim also highly praised the commentaries of Ibn Ezra on the Bible. His *hasidim*, of course, followed in his direction and he aroused the rage of the populist *hasidim* and the *mitnagdim* who looked malevolently on the renaissance of philosophy among the Pshis'cha *hasidim.*

Rabbi Simcha Bunim was beloved by the great scholars of that generation, such as Rabbi Akiva Eiger of Poznan and Rabbi Yaacov Lorbreboim of Lisa, the author of *Chavat Da'at (Opinion).* Although Rabbi Simcha Bunim put the study of the Talmud at the very center, and all of his *hasidim* were students of Torah, he opposed the ways of the *mitnagdim* of his generation who continued to learn and to teach in the *yeshivot,* in the same age-old ossified style. They mostly taught superficially and by rote, never reaching through to the inner spirit of Judaism.

When Rabbi Simcha Bunim was in Poznan, he said to the scholar, Rabbi Akiva Eiger,

> *There isn't any hope of establishing Judaism without the study of its inner spirit. The evil inclination that is in our time before the coming of the Messiah, resembles the candle that is about to be extinguished, which, in its final moments, the moment of its extinction blazes into a great but misleading light. Apart from the study of the Talmud, there is a need to deepen one's self as well into the inner spiritual aspects of Judaism.*

In one of Rabbi Akiva Eiger's interesting letters to Rabbi Bunim, he expressed his sorrow about the state of German Jewry in words that supported the viewpoint of Rabbi Simcha Bunim:

> *It amazes me. Thank G-d the majority of them here, in Poznan, revere G-d but still no one here has 'a fire in his belly' and there are no activists. I, myself, remain alone to wage the war for G-d. While in Poland, thanks to hasidism, the masses remained faithful to Judaism and are bound to the nation of Israel and its Torah.*

As a scholar of his generation, Rabbi Akiva Eiger felt the aching loneliness of his solitary position.

Besides the medieval scholarly literature, Rabbi Simcha Bunim admired the books of the Maharal of Prague, referring to the Maharal of Prague as his "teacher in Heaven". Although he did not study with him personally, the Maharal's teachings affected him deeply. Rabbi Simcha Bunim loved the fact that the Maharal's books excelled in logic and psychological depth. On an overt level, there is little of *Kabalah* in them and the *Zohar* hardly appears in them at all, but actually, all the basic concepts of the *Kabalah* are in the Maharal's books, without the use of special kabbalistic terminology. The *Kabalah* of the Maharal flows from logic and at first glance, it is hard to recognize its resemblance to *Kabalah*. Its style is simple and natural, from the heart, and captivating.

There is a great resemblance between the book, *Kol Simcha*, supposedly the words of Rabbi

Simcha Bunim, and the books of the Maharal. They have the same theoretical depth and straightforward logic, without the implied hints expressed in *Kabalah*, with *Kol Simcha* more closely resembling a style of logical discourse. There is also an obvious difference between *Kol Simcha* and the rest of hasidic literature. Similar to the Maharal's books, *Kol Simcha* is also more natural and simple and its words are spiced with parables and expressions taken from life.

Rabbi Simcha Bunim also greatly admired the book, *Mivchar Hapninim, (Choice Pearls)* of Rabbi Yedaya Hapnini, the Sephardic sage who believed in the philosophy of teaching with joy and whose style conflicted with that of the Rashba. *Mivchar Hapninim* excels in lofty moral ideas and is similar to the book of Proverbs. His sayings reflect a deep knowledge and understanding of life and are considered a precious gem among the *mussar* books. In its systems on the *midot*, there are many parallelisms between the teachings of Pshis'cha and *Mivchar Hapninim*.

Rabbi Simcha Bunim also learned a lot from the book *Tanna D'bei Eliyahu (Teachings from the House of Elijah)*. Every day he prepared a lesson for the study of this book, as the Pshis'cha *hasidim* loved the learning of *agada*—as expressed in *Tanna D'bei Eliyahu*—and its natural simplicity which is full of love of Israel.

From his early childhood, Rabbi Simcha Bunim was influenced by both his father and

Rabbi Mordechai Banet. His father, Rabbi Tsvi, the Magid of Vadislav, excelled in oratorical ability and lectured with straight forward logic and lofty ideas spiced with beautiful homilies. Similarly, Rabbi Mordechai Banet of Nikolsberg influenced him in the battle against assimilation, by his extreme righteousness, his pure scholarship, and his brilliance in Torah.

Perhaps one can compare Pshis'cha hasidism to Chabad since both of them demanded reflection and deep learning. As explained by the Rabbi of Liadi:

> *The essence of da'at, knowledge,e is not the knowing by itself, but that one should know the greatness of G-d from the mouths of writers and the mouths of books. The real essence of da'at is to deepen one's knowledge of the greatness of G-d...to immerse one's thoughts in it...The Torah is chochma, wisdom, binah, understanding, and da'at, knowledge.*

Because the discovery of the Divine revelation in the lower worlds is actually through observing and reflecting upon physically lower things, one should meditate on the physical planet earth which came into being out of nothing. In the same way, one should observe all the creatures, trees, animals, and *Ha-Midaber* (man, the one who speaks), so that from all this, G-d's divinity is revealed through the physicality of the world of *Asiyah*. In order to attain this meditation, a person actually has to become used to looking at things rationally.

These concepts are very close to the basic principles of Pshis'cha hasidism. Rabbi Simcha Bunim often quoted, "Lift up your eyes on high and see who created all of this." (Isaiah 40:26) But there is a fundamental difference between Chabad and Pshis'cha. According to Chabad, meditation is not just an instrument which affects only the improvement of *midot*, it is also a desired goal for its own sake. Rabbi Hillel of Paritch wrote,

> *The Rabbi of Liadi came up with a new insight, i.e. one needs to meditate on the Divine itself. One should connect with the Divine by examining the Divine, especially in our generation. It is a meditation on the deepest secrets of Divine manifestation ... even though it has nothing to do with the activating or inducing love and without a person's intention to reach love and awe. Through this meditation, one will eventually reach ahava, love, and yir'ah, awe, because in spite of the lack of that intention, the Divine light is drawn close as if closing in on evil until its eventual submission.*

However, according to Pshis'cha, the objective of

meditation is basically to arrive at good traits, especially the traits of truth and humility: "Know the Lord your G-d," they used to say in Pshis'cha, "so that you can arrive at the higher levels 'and consider it in your heart'." (Deut. IV:39)

All of Pshis'cha hasidism can be subsumed under one basic principle: a search for truth, in thought, in speech, and in deed. Every action that is not truthful and internalized within the soul is null and void. All things are important but only according to the measure of truth that is found in them. The demand for humility flows from this basic assumption.

A penultimate humility, the acknowledgment of one's own worth, is the first rule of ethical perfection. All the efforts of a person are in vain if he deceives himself and regards himself as a righteous person in his heart. He is far from the truth and there is no foundation for his Judaism. Rabbi Simcha Bunim attempted, by his preaching, to put Judaism on a prophetic basis, i.e. truth, loving kindness, and knowledge of G-d. His contribution is great in influencing the return to the early prophetic sources among the seekers of truth and the pursuers of justice that arose in Israel in the latter years.

Chapter 9

ACKNOWLEDGEMENT OF THE DIVINE

"Lift up your eyes and see who created all this." Exodus from Egypt and creation of the Heavens. Torah, and its value. The heart and the will. The thirst to know G-d.

"Hear O deaf ones, and see O blind ones!" (Isaiah 42:18) "How can this be," mused R. Mendel of Kotsk, who used to wonder why the prophet would turn to the deaf ones, commanding them to hear and the blind ones to see. Are they not disabled? Were their ears not closed up and their eyes not blind? But instead, the prophet turned to human beings whose ears were open but did not hear and whose eyes looked but did not see: "Deaf ones—you who make yourselves deaf—listen! Blind ones—you who make yourselves blind—look! Open your eyes. See and acknowledge G-d. As it is written, 'Lift up your eyes on high and see who created everything!'"

Because human beings are so accustomed to nature which is all around them, they think that this is the way it is supposed to be, that the sun rises and sets and the stars sparkle with their light. After a period of time, nature becomes habit and they are no longer at all interested in the Divine Creation. Not only do they not pay attention to the power of creation, they also ignore the majesty and splendour of creation itself. They live a life of total sensuality without experiencing any of the pleasure that comes from the spark of observance and reflection, without a ray of light from the joy and the love of the Creator and His creation.

According to the teaching of Rabbi Simcha Bunim of Pshis'cha, the goal of all creation is for the human to come to acknowledge the Divine, to know G-d. The acknowledgment of G-d comes from recognizing His works, and by recognizing all of creation. "The essence of worship is to know before whom one worships" and "from the heavens and the earth one grasps that G-d made them." This is the foundation of Judaism: "Lift up your eyes on high and see who created all this!" Look at the stars on high, at the moon, at the sun, reflect on the hosts of the sky, on its riches, on its splendour and recognize the Creator, that His is the majesty, the splendour and power.

The human is beloved with a special love, because he was created in the image of G-d. The human being is the crown of creation, and its ultimate purpose. All the understanding that is in the creation of all the worlds, from the loftiest to the lowliest, is reflected in the human. The human being has a power which includes both the higher and the lower worlds so that he can understand the other. Except for the human, all other creatures cannot grasp the other. Only he can. Because of man's intelligence, only he can grasp the wisdom of G-d and feel in his heart all its glory and splendour. When a human arrives at a high level, he can feel all the worlds in his very soul.

The "Holy Jew", the Yehudi, had a different perspective regarding one's knowledge of G-d. He believed that the foundation of Judaism is the exodus from Egypt, and taught with a focus that was similar to Rabbi Yehudah Halevi. The Yehudi interpreted that concept to mean that Judaism is based on the belief in the power of the Creator to change nature. Because of this, the exodus from Egypt is mentioned in the first of the Ten Commandments—"I am the Lord, your G-d who took you out of Egypt".

Legend tells us that the Holy Jew once removed all the moral levels and attainments of Rabbi Bunim till he was like a simple man who would pray from a prayer book, because the Yehudi believed that the essence of Jewish worship was to deeply implant simple faith. But Rabbi Simcha Bunim did not believe in merely simple faith. On this essential and fundamental point, Rabbi Simcha Bunim differed from his mentor, the Yehudi.

In contrast to that concept, Rabbi Simcha Bunim of Pshis'cha based the foundation of Judaism on the meditation of the verse, "Lift up your eyes on high and see who created all this." Rabbi Simcha Bunim felt that the worship of G-d evolves through deep understanding and intelligent mindfulness which is more important than simple faith and trust. To the faith of the heart and feeling, Rabbi Simcha Bunim added knowledge and intelligence. His teachings more closely resembled that of his friend, Rabbi Shneur Zalman of Liadi, who felt that one learned Torah only by way of *chochma, binah,* and *da'at.*

According to the words of Rabbi Simcha Bunim, one does not come to truly acknowledge G-d, by miracles and wonders that are outside of nature. All of creation is full of miracles. Nature by itself is a miracle and whoever has *da'at* sees the wonder that is in all creation and thus comes to the realization of the Divine. Every human who is complete in himself, whose *da'at* is broad and has additional *binah,* doesn't need a miracle. G-d made miracles and wonders in Egypt, because of their lack of *da'at* in exile. They needed plagues and wonders in order for them to come to the *da'at* of G-d. Therefore, there is no need for wonders for Israel today. Now they can learn to acknowledge G-d through extra meditation.

The Pshis'cha *hasidim* used to say: "signs and wonders are in the land of the descendents of Ham." They believed that meditation on the Divine Creation does not lead to the real objective if it is not also combined with plumbing the depths of the teachings of G-d. The Torah and nature are one. The world was created and is established only through the merit of Torah and through it, creation is constantly renewed. "The writing is the writing of G-d engraved on the tablets." (Exodus 32:15)

Rabbi Simcha Bunim believed that G-d is written in the Torah, and if the human being will purify himself sufficiently through Torah, he will recognize His Divinity, may He be blessed. Therefore, there is no need for investigation and wonders. A person will open his eyes and will see the truth only through Torah itself. When asked, "What does the learning of Torah resemble," Rabbi Bunim replied with an illustration:

> The Torah resembles a wagon made of strong planks joined together so tightly, that there is not even a crack and it is impossible to find even a slight slit. The traveler in this wagon is certain that he will not lose any of his belongings that are loaded on the wagon. No matter if it should seem that he is missing something, he will eventually find it after some searching.

So, too, is with the way of Torah. For one who engages in Torah, even if he falls sometimes from a moral level, even if he loses himself, his soul will immediately return and find it. The Torah will return him to the right path.

The heart which involves the desire of the soul, i.e. the will, is a very important sensibility. *Binah* by itself is not enough, if emotion is not joined with it. There must be a unity of brain and heart, a harmony of intelligence and emotion. Just as the brain needs the heart, so does the mind need desire or will. It unites both the means of penultimate knowledge and Torah, in the human's upward journey.

Rabbi Simcha Bunim explained the verse, "And he speaks the truth in his heart," (Psalms 15:2) this way: a leader and speaker of truth in his heart is a person who will speak the truth from the brain to the heart. A rule of Rabbi Simcha Bunim's teaching is that "the desire of the heart is at the beginning of each deed." When "...the human became a living soul," (Genesis 2:7) we recognized that the soul is the desire.

The intention of the verse, therefore, is directed toward the desire. Where there is a desire to a higher spiritual ascent, the deed comes by itself. However, whoever has in his heart an evil inclination, even though he did not actively commit the evil, is not looked at favourably by Heaven. Avraham, our father, would cause his son to be thrown into the furnace because he accepted the yoke of the kingdom of Heaven. When people accept upon themselves the yoke of the kingdom of Heaven, especially during the reciting of the *Shema*, although they are not actually sacrificing themselves and they are only performing it through the heart, it is considered as if they actively did do it.

Human beings who think that they can

come to know G-d through research, philosophy and intellectual insight, are mistaken. "The teachings of his G-d are in his heart." (Psalms 37: 31) There is no more suitable insight to attain the divine than through the heart. When a person purifies his traits, he will find the Divinity in his heart. It is specially designed to attain our holy Torah and His divinity. Read the verse: "From there you will seek G-d, your Lord, and if you pursue Him with all your heart and soul, you will find Him." (Deut. 4:29)

Rabbi Simcha Bunim explained it this way:

> *All the efforts to know G-d which comes only through wisdom and research will not reach the desired objective because those efforts do not flow from this other special source. Thus it is written 'From there,' i.e. from another place. 'From there you will seek G-d, your Lord…' A person may twist and turn to seek G-d through research and study but he loses his way because he is seeking it 'from there'. Suddenly a 'finding' appears upon his path in front of him, 'a ray of light', a wondrous light, which breaks through all his darkness, 'and you will find'. Why? 'Because you pursue Him with all your heart'; one needs to pursue G-d with all*

'your heart'.

For this reason, the Holy One, blessed be He, is concerned with the human heart. If it is clear and clean, and if the degree of cleanliness and clarity corresponds to the level of thirst for G-d and the inner aspiration to it, then the level of attaining the Divinity and the purification of the human is possible. It is only "the pain and thirst for *yir'ah* (awe) of G-d that causes the appearance of its light in the heart of the human."

Rabbi Simcha Bunim explains the verse from Psalms 63:3, "My soul thirsts for You... as I shall behold You in the sanctuary," in this way: "'My soul thirsts for You, G-d', corresponds to the degree of thirst that my soul has for G-d and relative to this value, I attain and behold the majesty of Your eternal sanctity '...As I shall behold You in the Sanctuary'."

Chapter 10

G-D AND MAN

The divine teaching and the soul of Pshis'cha. Description of the Divinity. The nature of man. The image of G-d. The soul. The desire and the intellect. Knowledge of G-d. The unity of the lower and upper worlds.

Unlike the hasidism of Chabad, which excelled in a rich literature, Pshis'cha hasidism, in principle, was opposed to the writing of books. Consequently, Rabbi Simcha Bunim did not leave a special book from which one could build a complete philosophical structure dealing with questions of the Divine and of man and the world. Only a few fragments remain in *Kol Simcha*, which according to the words of his students, in no way gives the full essence of his comprehensive world outlook. Other writings that appear in his students' notebooks are not enough to complete the picture. Nevertheless, from the few pieces that were salvaged, it is possible to peek into the primordial light of the Pshis'cha method and to enjoy the brilliance of its teaching.

The Pshis'cha point of view regarding the Divine and the human being is clearly derived from medieval Hebrew philosophy. Rabbi

Simcha Bunim was profoundly influenced by the deep psychological and penetrating analysis of the soul, as seen in Rambam's *Moreh Nevuchim (Guide to the Perplexed)* and Yehudah Halevi's *The Kuzari*, together with the works of the Maharal. These authors aspired to explain and harmonize the concepts of emotion and intellect through parables that were based on the lives of human beings. The secret of Rabbi Bunim's great influence was his familiarity with the human soul and that his teaching was based on a solid pedagogical foundation. The use of parables as a teaching tool was a common practice among Pshis'cha *hasidim* and Rabbi Simcha Bunim often used parables to get his point across.

In *Kol Simcha*, Rabbi Bunim spoke about G-d's great power and that this power is lofty and noble and beyond the comprehension of man. He quotes, "Who is like you, G-d, among the G-ds?" (Exodus 15:11) When a mortal king delegates some of his glory to another, he isn't king on that particular matter because on that matter, he has given his authority to the other. Nevertheless, that other person cannot wear the king's mantle, and cannot be called by the king's title. If he should do so, it would be perceived as a rebellion against the king's sovereignty. But the Holy One, blessed be He, even if He delegates His glory to another, blessed be He, He is still king on all that glory, because His kingdom is over everything and there is no place void of Him and no one other than Him, forever blessed.

Therefore, He is called "the King of Glory".

It's the same principle with the other traits and human practices which are attributed to G-d. G-d is lofty and beyond the comprehension of mortal people. One may praise a person who has some of G-d's attributes but still is not like Him. There certainly may be a person who has one or two of these attributes, nevertheless, there is no one person like G-d who has within Him all the attributes combined. This example alone does not allow for a comparison with G-d. There is none like Him in any way, not by any stretch of the imagination.

Another comparative example of G-d's uniqueness is human speech. Although human speech may be true, it does not have to be realized literally word for word: it is possible that a human may fulfill all his wishes, even though they may not be fulfilled exactly according to his utterances. For example, if a person will say to a friend, "Give me a cup of water!" and his friend gives him water in a goblet, he has fulfilled his entire request. Although the deed is slightly changed, the request is seen as fulfilled. What was actually said to him was the word "cup", not "goblet", but this is seen as a minor matter rather than an essential one, because in human speech, words that are not essential to one's intention may just pour out. In general, if a person says to do something, at the time of speaking, the thing is not yet done. The saying implies a promise to do the action. However, each word of Hashem, the blessed One, is total truth and is actualized for each specific purpose because, at the same time of the speech, the matter occurs immediately. There is nothing that G-d cannot do.

Although the Divine is exalted beyond our attainment, in the place of this greatness you will find His humility. G-d contracted Himself (*tsimtsum*), as it were, and created the physical world in a special order that is unfolding before us. Rabbi Simcha Bunim frequently quotes the Maharal:

> *The Creator, blessed be He, gave to all the creatures and all those in existence an ordered system within which they should behave. Hashem stamped it into all existence and called it 'nature'. Until the time that Avraham, our father, may he rest in peace, the world behaved according to nature. But, from the time that Avraham, our father, came into the world, it began to operate by miracles. Wasn't he thrown into the furnace and he was saved, etc.? All the plagues of the Egyptians and the parting of the Red Sea were all done by miracles. Thus G-d operated as such until He gave them the Torah. When Israel sinned, the world returned to operating according to nature and all the*

miracles were forgotten even though they themselves had been there. Because the world of miracles is higher than that of nature, human beings now had to learn through their intelligence and wisdom.

After the creation, which was made in a beautiful and splendid manner, G-d wanted to show His deeds to all those in existence. G-d said, "Let us make a human in our image and in our likeness." The likeness of the Divine reveals and contracts itself in the image of the human. Therefore, G-d created the human who is a power incorporating the upper and lower worlds, and is able to imagine all within his soul. The exaltation of the Divine is reflected within the soul as a part of G-d on High and a human, the earthling, (Adam) was derived from the earth (*adamah*), the lower world.

In reality, except for the human being, no creature can grasp the reality of anyone other than itself. This is the essence of man; that he will see, will understand, and will imagine the other. Thus we have the phrase, "Let us make man in our image and likeness...because only the one who is like Him can imagine it." (Maharal)

The Maharal believed that through consciousness and discernment, the soul of a human encompasses all creation, all the worlds, and all the wonder of formation. Because of this, in that verse, "Let us make man..." the names of the four worlds are mentioned: *atsilut* (closeness to G-d...communion with G-d), *briyah* (*vayibrah*, He created...world of intellect, creation), *yetsera* (*vayitsor*, He formed...world of emotion, formation), *asiyah* (*v'naaseh*, let us make...world of doing, physicality). The human will be able to feel all these worlds in his soul when he will be worthy of them.

The Maharal describes the origin of the soul in this way: the soul of man is important because it is extracted from under the Throne of Glory and derived from the One who formed creation. The soul of a human is complex and resembles in its mysterious marvels, the One from whom it is derived. But not all souls are equal. Each one has its own talents. "Forms of service vary according to the place from which the souls are extracted." Every single human deed impacts the development and evolution of the soul, until it openly appears in the world.

When a person needs something and wishes to pray to G-d to fulfill his need, the initial desire is in the heart, and afterward it is in thought. Letters of the alphabet are made up of thought, subsequently made into speech and then he prays. But this needs much study and the application of intelligence, and sometimes the desire can not spread itself into speech and not even into letters of thought. This is called a sense of "not yet". It is a boundary limit that does not go forth from the potential to action. Thus G-d promised them that He would answer them without any call. "Before they will call, I will answer." (Isaiah 65:24)

"The human being became a living soul." (Genesis 2:7) The soul of a human is recognized by his *ratson*, desire or will. The soul is the *ratson* and when the person is full of desire, then speech is easy for him. Desire activates and influences speech and deeds. However, the desire of a human does not always assure good behaviour.

Rabbi Simcha Bunim believed that a person might argue with his fellow man with all of his soul. He might speak impulsively and without deliberation because his words are only one-sided and uniform. The desire requires the mind to instruct it. The intelligent man judiciously weighs his words and keeps knowledge and understanding in his heart. His speech is led by the mind, sometimes in victory and sometimes in acknowledgement or in one of the traits that his mind has determined. In order for the soul to convey a specific goal, the feeling that is in the heart requires understanding.

Although the soul of the human is holy and is extracted from a higher source, there are many souls who are varied and different. Some of them are inclined to goodness from their very essence and some of them are inclined to evil. "Man is created in this world..." to be righteous in his deeds. The choice of a person to do evil or good is etched into the human. One person may be inclined in the depths of his heart towards doing good and another may be inclined in the depths of his heart towards the opposite, G-d forbid. However, if the evilly inclined does not yet act on his inclination and actually do the evil deed, he should not be punished. Punishment is only administered to evil acts, not evil thoughts. However, the evil one does not find favour in the eyes of the Lord and is not worthy of drawing close to the Divine.

Cain was angry at G-d because he was not aware that he had done anything wrong! He did not understand why his offerings were not as acceptable as the offerings of Abel. But G-d, the tester of the heart, knew that in his heart, Cain was inclined toward evil, and the heart is like a tool of raw material that receives shape from this way or that, like the letters of the Torah. The task of the mind is to conduct the heart to suit the Divine purpose, so that feelings will not spread their boundaries and become addicted to evil.

It is incumbent on a person to elevate his soul and to walk in the path of G-d's wisdom, from which he was derived. According to the teachings of Pshis'cha, the essence of the creation of all the worlds is the human, because the Creator created the world in His wisdom. He also created a human who will meditate on the works of the Creator and will see the immeasurable and incomparable greatness of His wisdom, and will praise, glorify, exalt, and extol the One who created all this.

Before there was sin, the human used to meditate constantly and was one with the divine wisdom within the soul, for all parts of the soul were meditating on G-d's wisdom, may He be exalted. We may conclude from this that the human also did not have a certain kind of knowledge, because all the essence of his soul was constantly clothed in this meditation. But when sin entered the world, even though a human can meditate sometimes on the greatness of G-d, this meditation is not constant. He now needs to have, awareness (*da'at*) and understanding (*binah*), so that he is aware that he is meditating. This is the goal of man—knowing, being mindful, and meditating on the greatness of the Creator.

It is incumbent on man to sanctify life, to purify it, to exalt it and to aspire to bond with G-d (*d'vekut*). The obligation of the soul is to unite itself with its Creator, *d'vekut*, and to incorporate within itself the wisdom of the Creator and His splendour. Therefore, he needs to know and understand the value of time—to know and spiritually understand that the present moments are really the only things that he actually possesses. "The number of days of the life of a human being is not accumulated." What was the past is no more. What is the future, doesn't yet exist. In life, one literally only has the present and one's actual deeds. Thus, time is accumulated by the same measures as that of deeds. If the deed is from Torah, *mitsvot* and complete truthfulness, then these will lead to an elevated life.

It is incumbent on the human, who is both

body and soul, to aspire to the fusion between the spiritual and physical worlds. Like "the neck which joins the head and the body of a person," *(Kol Simcha)* so too a person joins his soul to both "the higher and lower worlds." A person reaches this exaltation through Torah because the Holy One, blessed be He, does not have satisfaction from the world except from those who engage in Torah. Torah is the actual order of the world and all the worlds operate according to it.

Human aspiration needs to be the fusion of Torah, *yir'ah* (reverence) and *ahavah* (love). A person has to walk day and night with such complete faith and thought, never pausing even for a moment, so that all his deficiencies will fall away. "To know the greatness of the Holy One, blessed be He, who joins with people and who constitutes all the worlds and yet is not separated from this world even for one moment. That is the purpose of the creation of man."

Chapter 11

LOVE AND AWE

Yir'ah, higher fear and lower fear. Limited consciousness. Love and d'vekut (bonding). Joy and prophecy.

Through knowledge of G-d, a person comes to *yir'ah* of G-d. This *yir'ah* is not a fear of punishment, which is a lower fear, but it is *yir'ah*, a higher fear, a reverence of the exalted, the sensing of G-d's splendour and majesty, and the glory of His power. The essence of *yir'ah* is not that the human will fear "punishment of the body or that of finances, or that he will be afraid of punishment in this world or in Gehenim." But rather that "a man should be in awe of his Master, for He is the superior and essential Ruler and the root of all the worlds, and everything else around him is unimportant." (Foreword of *Zohar*, Bereshit 11:72)

According to the teaching of Rabbi Simcha Bunim of Pshis'cha, this special kind of fear and trembling, this *yir'ah*, is the foundation of Judaism. "The beginning of wisdom is *yir'ah* of G-d. It is an axiom that whoever does not have *yir'ah* is like an animal." (Ramatayim Tsofim p. 240) A person must constantly think on the greatness of the Creator, about the splendour of creation and His eternal power. He must deepen this thought to such a degree that he will understand and feel his own nothingness—the lowliness of his mind and his strength—in contrast to the greatness of the Creator and the eternal wisdom that is revealed in His creation.

According to Rabbi Bunim's words, "Every person in each moment must imagine the greatness of the Creator, blessed be He, as it is written: 'Lift up your eyes and see Who created all this!'"(Isaiah 40:26). A person therefore needs to know the greatness of the lower physical world, the greatness of the middle world, and the world above and the angels. Then slowly one can begin to advance little by little to *yir'ah* of G-d. That person will be amazed and will know the magnificence of the Creator, blessed be His name.

In the section Tochecha (Deut. 28:23), one can see man's "limited consciousness", his inability to grasp the splendour of the majesty of creation, and his lack of a breadth of vision in encompassing all the worlds in his mind. G-d cursed man with the most terrible curse, saying "Your heavens that are above your head will be brass, and the earth that is beneath you will be iron." In the name of his rabbi, Rabbi Moshe Leib of Sasov, Rabbi Simcha Bunim used to explain the verse in this way:

> *The heavens 'that are above your head' is the attainment of the heavens — the creation, the formation. It can become so bounded*

until the person will think that the heavens are like vessels upon his head and they will feel like brass, frozen, without any understanding of life, without grasping the eternal movement and infinity that is in creation. When a person meditates deeply on the wonders of creation and the eternal power, he experiences the nullification of his very being in the presence of the source of wonders and strength. When one sees and understands the greatness of the Creator and all the worlds and its creatures, he reaches love. Thus a person comes to yir'ah from which he ascends to the highest level — to the love of G-d and communion with Him, d'vekut. He clings to Him with much love and a deep inner communion, and feels that only in the shadow of His wings is it possible to find shelter and secure refuge. Yir'ah is the gateway to love.

In describing his existential sadness, Rabbi Simcha Bunim said,

When I look at this world, it seems to me to be a desolate wilderness. I see nothing in it, except for one forest and one human. I am alone in all the world. I don't have anyone to

*whom to turn except G-d, and
similarly, G-d does not have anyone
to whom to turn, except me!...The
ultimate goal of the human is
d'vekut; to be one with G-d and to
integrate one's self with Him; by
communing with G-d and
suppressing the ego, the self (bitul
hayesh)...Complete faith and
thought is required day and night
without a moment's pause, in order
to deepen one's self into it. Only in
this way will all the deficiencies
within him fall away.*

This thought can purify and elevate a
person to the highest level, for this is how a
person can become integrated into the light of
the Infinite and attain the world to come, the
world of *atsilut*, which is all spirituality and
communion with G-d.

According to Rabbi Simcha Bunim's
teachings, the essence of "the world to come" is
d'vekut, the communion of the soul with G-d, and
the nullification of the self for the sake of G-d,
may He be blessed. Communion with G-d
involves working continuously on our human
traits until one comes to a level of righteousness.
This level, the attainment of the world to come,
can be reached even in this world, by ascending
the steps of the ladder of moral perfection, i.e. by
pure traits, Torah, truthful behaviour, and
humility.

At the time of the giving of the Torah on Mt. Sinai, all Israel once merited this level because they were exalted to the level of a beloved people of G-d. When Israel was totally pure in the yearning of the soul, they were actually like angels. They, then, were able to come to the level of receiving Torah. Rabbi Simcha Bunim said that once we see intuitively that true *tsadikim* have a flame burning in their hearts, that flame becomes the total true yearning of the soul to unite with the Holy One, blessed be He. Their defilement ceases through the power of their service because they are so purified in all their souls and their traits.

When a person gets in touch with the infinite wisdom of creation, which is embodied on a small scale, as a microcosm in the human as "the image of G-d," he is filled with an infinite joy through the wisdom that the Creator has allotted to him, from His infinite understanding, *yir'ah*, the awe of exaltation fills the heart of a person with feelings of delight and happiness. From the awe of exaltation, a person comes to complete joy.

Rabbi Simcha Bunim's teachings were permeated by this joy. "It is the joy of wisdom and the preparation of prophecy...*yir'ah*, the awe of exaltation is wisdom."

Chapter 12

PRAYER

Prayer through the yir'ah of exaltation. Preparation for prayer. Suppression of strange thoughts. Private prayer. Prayer for the redemption of the Shechinah.

The prayer of a person should be saturated with the *yir'ah* of exaltation. He must understand the great value inherent in his conversing with G-d, and must prepare himself, so he can appropriately express the desires of his soul before the Creator of all things. Rabbi Simcha Bunim used a parable taken from *midrash* to explain the essence of prayer:

A king had a beloved and said to him, "Know that I will dine at your place. Go and prepare it for me." His beloved went and prepared an ordinary bed, an ordinary lamp and a table. They were simple things that really were not fitting for a king. When the king came, his servants came with him, surrounding him with golden lamps. When his beloved saw all the honour that was bestowed on the king, he was ashamed. He hid all the things that he had prepared for him because they were so ordinary. The king said to him, "Didn't I say to you that I am coming to dine with you? Why did you not prepare anything for me?" His beloved said, "I saw all this honour that came with you and I was ashamed so I hid all the ordinary utensils that I prepared for you." The king replied, "Believe me, I will reject all the utensils that I brought with me. For the sake of your love, I will not use these things, instead, I will use only yours."

The moral of the story is that the beloved of the king is the human being! He has been invited by the king who is the King of kings, to unite himself with Him in prayer. However, the human whose intelligence is limited, may not be capable of receiving the King properly, to pray the way one should. When he starts to visualize the greatness of the Creator and His splendour, when he sees with his mind's eye the glory of creation and its wonders, when he meditates on the glory of the King, i.e., His golden lamps and the abundance of spiritual light that is bestowed on the human from the Lord of all things, then he fills himself with the *yir'ah* of exaltation. He hides all his common objects, i.e. his senses and his lowly inclinations, lifting himself to an elevated consciousness and becomes filled with pure *yir'ah* for the sake of welcoming the King. And so the King, who favours him, says to him, "Believe me, for the sake of your love, I will use only your things!" Therefore, the foundation of prayer is the preparation for it.

Man should not approach the Torah and prayer with a heart full of lust and issues tied to the physical world. Before he begins to pray, he should cleanse his heart and his mind so that it is open only to holiness. Everyone must approach prayer according to his particular level of ability. He must strive to give his heart and his mind and all his limbs and his senses, as an 'offering'— separated and differentiated and for G-d alone. Only after the cleansing of even an iota of lust or of any such inclination, and by meditating on the greatness of the Creator, "will his mind and his heart be balanced. Then his prayer will flow from his heart and soul without any labour or pressure." This prayer is accepted in Heaven because it comes "from the depths of the heart and the power of the soul."

While praying, man should not cry too much, rather he should pray with joy. Weeping numbs the mind and interferes with a clear mind. "I will give you another illustration," Rabbi Bunim said:

> Once the leader of the service who was crying at the time of prayer, cried so much that his tears choked his throat and dimmed his eyes so that his lips were unable to enunciate the words of the prayer properly. Someone said to him, "Instead of crying so much so that the words come forth from your mouth crushed and unclear, why don't you pray with joy and enunciate the words clearly?"

In general, hasidism teaches one to elevate those thoughts to the higher source—to the love of Hashem, because all the lower traits have their foundation and roots in those of the highest traits. Therefore, when a person directs his thoughts to their roots, he can make them holy and exalt them to a very high level. However, according to Rabbi Simcha Bunim, this path is dangerous and is meant only for a chosen few holy people. For the majority of worshippers, this path is not recommended.

Rabbi Simcha Bunim had a different perspective concerning 'strange thoughts'[3] that arise during the time of prayer. He taught that one should not push away the strange thoughts. Instead, he taught his *hasidim* to nullify them by mindfulness and knowledge. For example, when he, Rabbi Simcha Bunim, once overheard someone at the wall praying with great strength, he understood that he was putting out so much effort in an attempt to oust his strange thoughts. Rabbi Simcha Bunim waited until after the prayer and said to him: "I advise you, my son, listen to me, and it will help you. When these strange thoughts occur to you, such as a horse or the like, don't push it away but rather confront it. Stop the thoughts only a little. Then clarify its nature and that indeed it is only a horse or the like. Behold, truthfully you will find that there is nothing there and the thoughts will be null and void."

This is like the saying, "if your enemy is

---

[3] generally interpreted as thoughts of a sexual nature (G.L.)

hungry, feed him bread." Without totally pushing them away at once, a person can accomplish this gradually and with discernment. This negation of 'strange thoughts' is the basic principle for many of the behaviours of the *hasidim* of Pshis'cha and Kotsk. Hasidism also used this process of nullification in relationship to deeds and bad traits between man and man. They were always practicing to negate evil, to make it null and void, and to draw out its evil sting.

Prayer does not have to be only in a synagogue, but rather in every place and in whatever language one might wish to pray. Pshis'cha *hasidim* believed that, in prayer, the heart is the most important thing. "The Merciful One requires the heart," they said. They consequently believed in the importance of spontaneous prayer. In every place and time, when a person's heart fills itself with the desire to pray, he should pray. For this reason, Pshis'cha *hasidim* were not strict about praying communally. Therefore, they also used to delay the time of prayer, only praying when they felt ready, when they experienced the *kavanah*, intention of the heart and the *yir'ah* of exaltation.

Rabbi Simcha Bunim quoted, "A human should always be G-d-fearing both in private and in public, inwardly and externally, acknowledging the truth and speaking truth in his heart." He usually explained the quotation on prayer, "he got up early and spoke" in this way:

"Only the human who prepares himself for prayer by cultivating a pure heart and speaks truth from his heart, 'will get up early and will speak.'" Therefore, man should pray early in the morning, a prayer at its felt time. The objective of prayer is for a human to pray for divine revelation and redemption of Israel from exile.

Rabbi Simcha Bunim deemed *da'at*, knowledge of G-d, a primary objective. He believed that when knowledge of G-d in the world expands, people will also be freed from their physical troubles. He gave the following parable to illustrate this point:

The son of the king misbehaved and his father banished him from his house. He wandered in remote villages and earned his living by hard physical labour in order to sustain himself. After a period of time, he completely forgot his origin and his roots. From so much work and poverty, he turned into a coarse peasant. Once, the king wanted to check up on his son, and he sent one of his closest confidantes to see what kind of person his son had become. This person found the son in a tavern, drunk. He engaged him in conversation and transmitted to him, in the name of the king, that he is ready to fulfill any heartfelt requests if he will return to the king with repentance in his heart. The vulgar son of the king said, "The request of my heart is only one thing: I would like some warm wool clothing and good shoes." Instead of requesting material things, such as bread and clothes, it would have been better if the king's son had asked for a complete redemption. The material requests would then have fulfilled themselves.

Chapter 13

TRUTH AND INTENTION

The greatness of virtue. Inner and outer truth. The sin of lying. The sin of imitation. Deeds according to personal training. Strict people and their strictness. A parable for those who afflict themselves.

One of the principles of Pshis'cha hasidism is that all of a human's life, his entire actions, his words and his thoughts, should be imbued with the spirit of truth. The nature of truthful people is that they are unbiased. They are led only by the impartiality of truth. It is praiseworthy for knowledgeable people to clarify and to discern the truth from the lie and not go from one extreme to another. They will look at both sides of a situation, seeing all the complexities, and select a middle way. That is the attribute of truth, an attribute of Jacob, and of Holy Scripture. The high value placed on truth in our Torah is great. Rabbi Simcha Bunim said that we can see this because we did not find a warning to distance one's self from any sin other than the sin of lying: "You should distance yourself from a false word." (Exodus 23:7)

Our lack of the trait of truthfulness almost always is one of self-deception. In each person's eyes, his life appears whole and pure, without any blemish or sin. "I can return all the sinners of Israel to *tshuva*," said Rabbi Simcha Bunim, "but only on the condition that they will not lie." At the conclusion of every holiday and at the time of departing, he used to say to each of his *hasidim*, "I request of you only one thing. Promise me to fulfill it." "I promise," each *hasid* responded. "I am asking you not to speak lies!" said Rabbi Simcha Bunim. "In the place where truth resides there is no place for sin."

Rabbi Simcha Bunim once asked one of his *hasidim* about the essence of hasidism. "Hasidism is acting according to the lenient spirit of the Law," the *hasid* answered him. "Yes," said Rabbi Simcha Bunim, "it is written in the Torah, 'Do not deceive one another.' (Leviticus 25:17) However, the *hasid* who acts according to the lenient strictures of the Law must also not deceive himself. On a superficial level, it may appear as if every person acts truthfully. When a man knows himself and can be truly self-honest, then *tshuva* can occur."

However, Rabbi Simcha Bunim believed that all the liars in the world are prepared to prove with clear 'evidence' that all their deeds and their words are pure truth. The reason for this is that people often fail to see the truth in speech. In everyday speech, it is possible to justify every kind of lie and deceit so that even honest people do not usually have the strength to confront those words and deeds. The tongue is the clothing that hides from our eyes the truth as it really is. Only when people will realize that one must see truth as a hidden and secret thing, and that one has to pursue it from its many covers and garments, only then will the knowledge of truth be spread among people. "Behold truth which you desire is in the concealed parts." (Psalms 51:8) Because self-deception is so pervasive, Rabbi Simcha Bunim felt that one has to pursue truth in the depths, in the secrets of the soul, and in the hiddeness of the heart.

Another reason for the spread of the lie is that people stopped seeing the lie as a sinful thing. Someone who repeatedly transgresses regards it as permissible. In spite of all the warnings of the Torah and ethical precepts, people no longer understand how great is the sin of lying. The objective of Pshis'cha hasidism was to remind the whole world that lying is a sin and that the lie is the most serious transgression in the Torah.

Everyone knows that fornication is a sin. The adulterer will never justify himself, by claiming it is a good deed. Rabbi Simcha Bunim wished that the lie would become as serious a thing in the eyes of the world as adultery. "Only then," he said, "will redemption come to the world and the days of the Messiah will come."

All human deeds and especially worship of G-d should not be an imitation, but rather it should come from the depths of truthful intention. This emphasis on truth flows throughout the teachings of Pshis'cha hasidism. When a person does a *mitsvah* or prays just because his friends or his rabbi prays, what is lacking in his actions is the point of independent truth. Every *mitsvah* that the person practices has to come from his own inner awareness and the ability of his own soul, or, in the language of hasidism, "according to the root of his soul."

Rabbi Simcha Bunim used to say:

> *If they were to suggest to me that I will be great like Avraham, our father, and Avraham will be like me, I would not agree. Because what would the Holy One, Blessed be He, gain if sightless Bunim, would be like Avraham, our father, and Avraham, our father, would be like sightless Bunim! For this very reason, in parashat Naso, in the dedication of the mishkan (Numbers 7:30), the specific names of all the chiefs are mentioned and their offerings are also mentioned individually, such as, 'this is an offering of... his offering was one silver dish,' etc. (Numbers 7:30) Instead of writing a sentence including all the chiefs, the intention was to show that each chief even though he gave his offering in the same order as that of his peers, in spite of that, he offered*

> *it in his own special inner way according to his soul. Therefore, the human should learn from the creations of the Creator and should walk in His ways.*

The same way that the Holy One, Blessed be He, created human beings, hundreds of millions of them, and not one of their faces resembles another, so a person should behave. No one deed should resemble another's. Each action and thought should flow from an inner freedom, from the essence of the soul. The Holy One, Blessed be He, hates imitation.

In Deut. 18:14, it is stated, "But you, not thus (*lo ken*) has the Lord your G-d made you." (Fox translation) Rabbi Simcha Bunim explained the verse in this way: "You are a human, do not do your action only in a prescribed way (thus, *lo ken*)." It means, do not worship your G-d in a fixed format, in a pre-ordained order. A person whose deeds flow from the core of his soul does not worship G-d in a set way.

Every *mitsvah* has a hidden secret. "To Torah and *mitsvot* there is a hidden interior." For this reason, human deeds and the commandments of the Torah are important only if they are done with *kavanah*, (intention). The *mitsvah* on its own is an external deed, i.e. physical. According to Rabbi Simcha Bunim's language, "The *mitsvah* is the instrument that G-d gave to us for the *sod*, the secret that is accomplished only by the *mitsvah* with *kavanah*.

114

The *mitsvah* is only the external manifestation of the hidden intention. Rabbi Simcha Bunim further explained,

> *The mitsvah is mystery and must be accompanied by binah, understanding. It is the light…and therefore, binah is greater than the deed. The essential aspect is binah, the inner intention that is hidden in the deed. Man is obligated to perform the mitsvot, which he must do with an inner vitality. If they don't have an inner vitality, they will not rise up to heaven.*

"Knowledgeable people who do not want to do *mitsvot* senselessly and by rote are praiseworthy," wrote Rabbi Simcha Bunim, "even if the matter itself is a good thing, because they had the knowledge and knew how to differentiate and clarify the truth from falsehood." Anyone who performs his deeds without *kavanah* and without the primordial light that is in the *mitsvot*, distances himself from the truth. He holds to lies and pride and thinks only that people will praise him.

"It is known," said Rabbi Simcha Bunim "that the trait of modesty is very praiseworthy. As it is said: 'To walk modestly with the Lord, your G-d.' (Micah 6:8) Therefore, performing *mitsvot* publicly can lead one to pride, G-d forbid." For this reason, Pshis'cha *hasidim* avoided performing *mitsvot* in public, thinking that they might be enticed by pride or arrogance. For example, on the night of Yom Kippur, sometimes they did not pray in public. They did not say *Kol Nidre*, but rather, everyone prayed for himself in a simple evening service.

They were especially immersed in meditation and introspection. During the weekdays, a Pshis'cha *hasid* often used to walk around with a cigarette in his mouth, absorbed in the scholarly study of *Gemara*, and *Tosefot*, with an expanded consciousness. At twilight, he rolled all his prayers into one, i.e. *shacharit*, *mincha*, and *maariv*.

This was Pshis'cha *hasidim's* way of protesting against the rest of the *hasidim* and the *mitnagdim* for whom simple straightforward observance of the *mitsvot* was most important, while they often neglected the *kavanah* and the inner meaning of Torah. "Pshis'cha hasidism," Rabbi Yitschak Meir of Gur said, "teaches that a person should not do anything through his external parts, the essence is only through interiority—through his heart and his knowledge. And this inwardness will awaken him to the external deed."

Among the Pshis'cha *hasidim*, there was no place for all kinds of rigid observers and embellishers of *mitsvot* and for those people who often fasted a lot. When it occurred that such an individual came among the Pshis'cha *hasidim*, they immediately investigated and rebuked him for his external superficiality, and said that his inwardness was deficient. They said, "Only a person who is not completely in awe of G-d needs to have many fences. Therefore, restrictions and fences are heaped upon him. But for the person whose heart is clearly in *yir'ah* of G-d, there is no such need for this. And this is like it was written earlier, 'You who did cleave to the Lord, your G-d' (Deut. 4:4) and afterwards, 'you shall not add anything.' (Deut. 4:2) You will not need 'fences'. Where there is a breadth of knowledge there is no need for restrictions and 'fences'."

When they related to Rabbi Simcha Bunim about the praises lavished on a particular man who completes the Book of Psalms every day, he remarked: "If in half the psalms it is said: 'But they sought to beguile him with their mouth and they deceived Him with their tongues,' (Psalms 78:36) all the more so is the person who finishes all of it."

For several years an ascetic afflicted himself with torments. He once complained to Rabbi Simcha Bunim about his bad luck in achieving the Revelation of Elijah, i.e. the revealed appearance of Elijah. He had already done all that was written in the "holy books" in order to reach the level of Revelation of Elijah and still he did not achieve it, in spite of all his efforts. "I will illustrate the point with a parable," answered Rabbi Simcha Bunim.

The Besht, may his memory be for a blessing, when he wanted to travel

*to a particular place by a miraculous
means, he gave the impression of
harnessing his magical horses to his
wagon and thus he went on his way.
People used to feed their horses at
each station so that they could
travel further... However, on this
miraculous fantasy journey, they
did not feed them fodder. The horses,
which were used to eating at each
station, were surprised by that.
They went on traveling, flying in
the wind, from station to station
and were not given any fodder.
Finally, the horses came to the
conclusion that they were not horses
but rather people. They thought that
when they will come to the main
station they will be served human
food. However, they were so
astonished when they saw that in
the main station they again were
not given food, but instead they
continued to fly as if "on wings of
eagles." Thus the horses decided
that they were not people either, but
rather angels. And the proof is that
they didn't have a need for either
fodder or food. However, when the
Besht came to his destination and
the horses who pretended to be
angels were taken to the stables,*

they began to overeat and drink excessively like real horses.

The moral of the story is: the ascetic, who sits continuously fasting for days, without food or drink, thinks that he has already reached the degree of an angel. However, when after the fast, they give him food, he overeats and drinks to excess like the horses, yet still he wants to merit "The Revelation of Elijah".

Chapter 14

HUMILITY

Assumed humility and inner humility. Humility of discernment. A parable about humility in Pshis'cha. Humility brings one to communion with G-d.

The trait of *anavah*, humility, holds an important place in the hasidism of Pshis'cha. They placed great value in implanting deeply the trait of humility. Hasidism, in general, had made humility the main foundation of their philosophy. However, Pshis'cha *hasidim* focused even more profoundly on it and were highly critical of the kind of humility practiced by the general hasidic community. They stated that the general practice was incomplete because they did not take it to its highest degree.

Over and over again, Pshis'cha teaching emphasized that the power and root of evil is arrogance. The degree to which this arrogance assumes the appearance of holiness is its most dangerous aspect. A *hasid* may think of himself as being humble and lowly. For example, he may not be angry with anyone. He may not pride himself above the public or be self-glorifying. However, for Pshis'cha *hasidim*, even this was not humility. They called this behaviour 'politeness'. Since people know that pride is loathsome in the eyes of others, they themselves, therefore, behave with this kind of superficial humility. "However, such humility is merely pride," say Pshis'cha *hasidim*. "A feeling of egotism in him teaches him to behave humbly, so that he will please people."

Humility, according to Pshis'cha, flows from *da'at*, awareness, and *binah*, understanding. When a person pictures in his mind the magnificence of creation and the splendour of its glory: of the moon, the sun, and the majesty of stars, the seas, the wilderness, the different lands and the myriad faces of people and their diverse ideas; when one imagines the *olamot*, the spiritual worlds, and the *sephirot*, spheres of emanations of G-d; when the capability and eternal power of the Creator, the Holy One Blessed be He, is obvious; then he feels his insignificance, his nothingness, and he eventually becomes lowly in his mind. Thus, he reaches an elevated level of pure humility, the humility of *da'at* and *binah*.

This humility is totally dependent on the inner state of a person and not on his external behaviour. A person can demean himself by every sign of lowliness and still remain prideful in his inner soul. True humility goes beyond priding himself over others. Rabbi Simcha Bunim once said,

> Sometimes a man isolates himself in the depths of the forest, in order to worship G-d silently far away from people and their noises and tumult. However, if only once a brief feeling

> *of smugness sneaks into his heart when he sees a person pass who sees his retreat and his solitude—then all his worship is the worship of a lie. Even if there is in his heart only a smidgeon of pride, honour, or arrogance—he is prideful.*

The higher, pure humility flows from *da'at* and from meditation. The *hasidim* told of a *hasid* of Rabbi Uri of Strelisk who once came to Pshis'cha. "What did Rabbi Uri teach you?" Rabbi Simcha Bunim asked him. The *hasid* answered,

> *Our teacher used to teach us about the trait of humility. Every hasid who came to him, whether he were a great scholar, or a rich and respected person or not, had to be a drawer of water. He had to bring two pails of water through the street before the eyes of all the passers by, so that he would learn to be modest in spirit and to be humble.*

Rabbi Simcha Bunim said to him,

> *One also teaches the trait of humility here, but in a different way. I'll illustrate it with a parable: A king sent three people to prison, two were wise and one was a fool. The three of them were put in a dark cellar, in which daylight did not*

penetrate at all. Food was lowered to them through a hole, and the three prisoners divided up the food between them. But the fool couldn't put the food in his mouth, because he wasn't used to the new utensils of the prison. Instead of eating the food, he overturned the utensils and threw the food. One of the wise prisoners, who couldn't bear to see the suffering of the fool, took care of him. Each time that they lowered the food, he gave him the utensils in his hand and he, himself fed him all the meals. In contrast to this, the second prisoner did not interest himself in the situation of the fool. As several days passed, the feeder lost his patience and was angry at his friend, the wise one, who was not helping in the feeding of the fool. 'My friend' the second wise one answered him regarding anger, 'while you were working hard to feed him, I am sitting and thinking all day of plots to break through the wall of the prison so that daylight could enter and the fool will see for himself how to put food in his mouth.'

The moral of the story is this: The rabbi of Strelisk made his *hasidim* draw water in order to instil in them humility, while Rabbi Simcha Bunim of Pshis'cha thought about how to instil in them the light of discernment and awareness so that humility will emerge from within.

In Pshis'cha, there was no place for elitists, for those who considered themselves 'the beautiful people', pillars of society. These were the people who put on airs and felt pleasure when people honoured them. The young students of Rabbi Simcha Bunim often used to aim their sharp ridicule at these Jews. They used to tease them with verbal barbs descending right into their very gut, crushing them till they were dust. So great was their zeal for humility, they permitted themselves to even mock and belittle their friends in order to humble their spirit. They were constantly trying not to overestimate each other's virtues for fear that might possibly lead to a level of arrogance.

The way of Rabbi Simcha Bunim took a less harsh form. He would humble the prideful among his *hasidim* with barbs of the learned. He cited the *Chazal* saying, "Everyone who flees from honour, honour will pursue him." In contrast to the saying of *Chazal*, one *hasid*, a 'beautiful Jew', complained to Rabbi Simcha Bunim, that even though he personally flees from honour, honour does not pursue him. Rabbi Simcha Bunim replied, "Actually, you flee from honour but every now and then you look behind you to see if indeed honour is already pursuing you."

Humility flows from knowing the verse, "For though G-d is exalted, He sees the lowly." (Psalm 138:6) Rabbi Simcha Bunim interpreted it in this way: "One cannot see, i.e. grasp the exaltation of G-d, if one is not humbled in his own mind. Therefore, a descent is needed in order to ascend to it." It is impossible to come to know G-d without a move toward one's inner being and a genuine humbling of one's self. Nevertheless, according to the teaching of Pshis'cha, one should not overdo one's own humbling. The humbling process also needs to be kept in moderation. One should not belittle one's self to such a degree as to nearly come to despair and sorrow.

Rabbi Simcha Bunim said, "Every person should try to remember two sayings, 'I am dust and ashes,' (Genesis 18:27) and 'for my sake the world was created.'" (Mishna Sanhedrin 4:5) At one time a person might use the first saying and at another time he might use the second saying. The humility which raises a person to a meaningful life and joy of the soul is the only desirable one. "This humility," said Rabbi Simcha Bunim, "causes a void in the heart of a person. The pride that used to dwell in the heart exits and leaves behind it an empty space. The aim of the true *hasid* is to put into the empty place the love of G-d, *d'vekut*, communion with the Creator of the world." According to Pshis'cha, "humility originates from *da'at*, knowledge whose objective is *d'vekut*, communion with G-d."

Chapter 15

T'SHUVA — REPENTENCE

The power of the impact of t'shuva.
The greatness of the virtue of
t'shuva. Inner t'shuva. T'shuva
through joy.

In the teachings of Pshis'cha, *t'shuva*, the
ability to transform the wrong-doer and sinner
into a *tsadik* and a spiritual leader of a
generation, is very important. Rabbi Simcha
Bunim once said,

> *If only a baal t'shuva knew how*
> *great is the power of t'shuva.*
> *Merely thinking about it lifts his*
> *soul to the level of a tsadik. The baal*
> *t'shuva would rejoice greatly*
> *because he merited a release from*
> *darkness to a great light. But*
> *Heaven will not show him this*
> *authentic degree of spirituality,*
> *because it could compromise his*
> *sense of choice and then he might*
> *completely reject this world and its*
> *vain assumptions.*

Rabbi Simcha Bunim believed intensely in
his ability to influence his followers and elevate
them to a high spiritual level, to the level of
t'shuva. One of his students, the *maskil*, Yitschak

from Yazs, recalled that Rabbi Simcha Bunim once claimed he was capable of rehabilitating every wrong-doing Jew, saying, "I am not a rabbi. But anyone around me who does not do *t'shuva* is accountable and will be judged!" Another time, he declared, "When I take a soul in my hand, to wash and cleanse it, ounces of blood flow from it." He strongly believed in his ability to go into the depths of a person's soul, to its hidden places, and pull out all its evil.

His *hasidim* tell that, once Rabbi Simcha Bunim sat with them and engaged in discussing matters of *t'shuva*. He arose from his place and exclaimed passionately, "Rambam said, 'and what is *t'shuva*? …that the sinner will leave sin and will remove it from his thoughts and will decide that he will not do it again. And G-d, the One who knows the mysteries, will testify for him that he will never return to this sin.'" Then Rabbi Bunim continued, "Anyone who does not do *t'shuva* like this doesn't have a place near me!" The *hasidim* were shocked and in panic fled from their Rabbi. Only Rabbi Mendel of Kotsk remained and said, "I don't have the strength to flee."

Rabbi Simcha Bunim also said to his *hasidim*,

> *Listen and I will teach you the way of t'shuva. One does not come at t'shuva through crying and rolling about in the dirt. Know that because of t'shuva and remorse, some people*

are pleading and crying, 'Pardon us!' However, immediately after the confession, they plead for greatness. This has no value whatsoever. For this reason even though we say the confession three or four times every day, the Messiah still does not come.

The matter of *t'shuva* is like this: at the time of the confession when one will say, "We have sinned," the person should recognize that he is neither fit nor worthy of any favour at all. On the contrary, he is worthy of punishment and hard afflictions. At the time of the confession, he should accept all the afflictions in the world and surrender himself and his soul to G-d, May He be Blessed, and know that G-d may do to him whatever He wishes, within a context of total love. The person's ego becomes null and void and he accepts whatever judgment will be meted out to him. It should not occur to him that he might achieve the high level. Only when he actually reaches this level of contrition, G-d willing, the Blessed One will send him a new light and the following verse will apply to him: "create a pure heart for me, O G-d." (Psalm 51:12) The confession should only be done in this manner.

T'shuva is done by acknowledging that his value is truly diminished; that he is not worthy of any virtue and importance; and that only the Holy One, Blessed be He, brings him close to Him with much compassion in the fullness of loving kindness. The actual sin is not so terrible. Not every person merits standing trial. The real sin begins at the time when it is possible for a person to do *t'shuva* and he does not. "The imagery of man's heart is evil from his youth." (Genesis 8:21) When he gets used to sinning and is not remorseful, he becomes a criminal and a sinner.

There are some who think that by observing the commandments and doing good deeds, they will atone for their sins. However, according to Pshis'cha, *mitsvot* and good deeds only save one from punishment. First and foremost, one needs to feel shame for his sin. One needs to feel revulsion for his transgression to such a degree that he will feel total heartbreak about his ethical descent.

According to the teachings of Pshis'cha, during the time he dwells on his sin, the bitterness in his heart is so great that it nearly vents his spleen. He is overcome by it all. "*T'shuva*," said Rabbi Simcha Bunim, "is the killing of the ego." This means a person must feel as if he lost all the essence of his life by his sinning. He must sense the emptiness that dwells in his heart from the day that he was caught in the net of the evil inclination, and feel his complete nothingness and submit to the complete negation of self, as if he himself were killed. When a person comes to that degree of *t'shuva* and feels such bitterness, he has to be careful that he will not continue on to grief and despair. Through the darkness of sin, he will come to see the light of *t'shuva*. It brings one to the throne of Glory.

The atonement of sins comes only through the process of *t'shuva*. *T'shuva* is not only by speech. Real change occurs only through an interior process. It comes from the innermost part of a person, "from the depths of the heart" (*mei'amka d'liba*). *T'shuva*, before the Holy One Blessed be He, is more important than good deeds and Torah as the deed is an external matter to a person, and it is possible that something about it will be lacking. Words of Torah are not constantly close to a person, because at a time that a human is not lucid in his mind, words of Torah may also be lacking. But the potential for *t'shuva* is in the "essence of a person" and is constantly there.

Every time that a person will turn his heart to grow closer to G-d, Blessed be He, he will pray before Him and pour out his words to Him, and G-d will answer him. And the Holy One, Blessed be He, does not ask sacrifices and offerings of man but rather qualities dependent on the essence of a person—*t'shuva*, a process "from the depth of the heart" (*Mei'amka d'liba*).

Chapter 16

A TSADIK

The value of the tsadik within Pshis'cha hasidism. The tsadik in popular hasidism. Chabad and Pshis'cha. A parable of R. Isaac son of R. Yekilsh. The tsadik as a spiritual guide. The revitalization of hasidism.

Like hasidism in general, Pshis'cha hasidism acknowledged the existence of an elevated man, crowning his head with a garland of greatness. According to its teaching, the *tsadik* is above the rest of the people who surround him. His elevation is essentially in his ability to raise all physical things to their highest spiritual potential, to draw out the "holy sparks" from every secular deed, and to connect the physical world to the spiritual one. The *tsadik* directs all his physical deeds for the sake of G-d. He stresses the spiritual, the Divine that is within all his deeds. Even when he hears simple words from "lesser people", his thoughts are not stuck in that direction. On the contrary, he draws out a "hint of *chochma*" from them because "all the stories of this world are Torah for him." A sense of *d'vekut* pervades all the movements and activities of the *tsadik*.

The *d'vekut* of *tsadikim* is similar to that of

all Israel standing at Mt. Sinai. True *tsadikim*—according to the teaching of Pshis'cha—have such a flaming fire in their hearts till there is no ego, only a yearning for G-d, Blessed be He. They become so purified through the power of their heartfelt worship that whatever foulness exists within them is extinguished. Their souls hover in the higher worlds and they enjoy the splendour of the *Sh'china*. Thus they reach the level of receiving the Torah, like real angels.

A *tsadik* who reaches this level is above time and place, and even if he descends to an impure place, he is not spoiled by it. His soul cleaves to G-d and remains pure. He can also do things that the rest of the people are forbidden to do, if it is for the sake of the *mitsvah*. He is permitted to do transgressions, if it is for the sake of G-d. For example, "*Tsadikim* can even make a feast which could be considered like a fast."

However, in spite of the common understanding of the characteristics of a *tsadik*, there was a fundamental difference regarding the status of the *tsadik* between popular hasidism and Pshis'cha hasidism. According to the teaching of general popular hasidism, "the people who travel to the *tsadik* to cleave to him, are the branches from the root of his soul. In their approach to him, he raises and entwines their souls upwards from their roots. They are his sparks that need to be raised up. This is the way of the *tsadikim* who raise all the sparks and all the souls who fall below. He becomes one with all of them to cleanse and purify them." In general, the *tsadik* of popular hasidism occupies the most important place, as the *tsadik* is the central point through whom all the world is nurtured, both in the spiritual and physical.

In contrast to this, Pshis'cha hasidism essentially emphasizes the obligations of the *hasid*, rather than the greatness of the *tsadik*. The *tsadik* is seen only as the spiritual guide for the *hasidim*, who are aspiring to raise themselves up. The responsibility rests solely upon the *hasid*.

Rabbi Simcha Bunim from Pshis'cha once described the difference between his system and the contrasting system of his opponent, Rabbi Meir Halevi from Apta, in this way. Whereas popular hasidism placed great value on the *tsadik*, Pshis'cha hasidism mainly emphasized the self obligation of the *hasid* and therefore, put the heart as most important. Therefore, Rabbi Simcha Bunim considered the heart the most important organ of the human being. Rabbi Meir, however, considered the shoulders as the most important part of the body, namely the broad shoulders of the *tsadik*, which were capable of carrying the *hasid*.

Rabbi Simcha Bunim objected so strongly to the exaggerated value placed by *hasidim* on the *tsadik* that he once said that, for this reason alone, it would be worthwhile to completely cancel hasidism and return to the way of the *mitnagdim*. The source of his objection stems from the days of the "Holy Jew" who also saw this dependency on the *tsadik* as the beginning of the degeneration of hasidism. In Pshis'cha, they feared that so much dependency on the *tsadik* would diminish the personal efforts of *hasidim* to aspire to spiritual exaltation.

In this matter, Pshis'cha hasidism resembled the hasidism of Chabad. Rabbi Shneur Zalman of Liadi also diminished the value of the *tsadik* in order to raise up his *hasidim*. The *hasidim* tell that, when Rabbi Shlomo from Karlin wanted to settle in the city of Bishinkovits, in the Vitebsk District, he sought the consent of the rabbi of Liadi. The Rabbi granted his request, but only on condition that it would not be said that the *tsadik* must carry his sheep. On the contrary, he added, it should be explained to them that each person must be individually responsible and accountable for his soul. They must adopt *mitsvot* and good deeds and not rely at all on other mere mortals.

There is a famous and beautiful parable told by Rabbi Simcha Bunim of Pshis'cha, concerning the relationship of Pshis'cha *hasidim* to the *tsadik*: The rich and famous Rabbi Isaak, son of Rabbi Yelkish from Krakow, once had a dream. In the city of Prague, near the bridge abutting the king's palace, a great treasure whose value was immeasurable was hidden in the earth. Because the dream was repeated several times, he decided to travel there to look for the treasure. When Rabbi Isaak came to Prague and wanted to dig, in order to extract the treasure, the armed policemen who were standing on guard for the palace, told him that it was forbidden to approach the palace without special permission from the king. Rabbi Isaak walked around in front of the palace for several days without a solution, wondering what to do, because he did not wish to reveal the secret of the treasure to the king's guards. Finally, when he realized there was no alternative, he approached the head of the guards and revealed to him everything that was in his heart and asked his advice. The head of the guards heard his words, laughed and said, "Who believes in futile dreams and even spends money on them? Look, I dreamed that a buried treasure of precious gems and jewels is concealed in the room of one Jew in Krakow, whose name is Rabbi Isaak, son of Rabbi Yelkish. Should I travel to Krakow to search for the treasure on the basis of the dream?" When Rabbi Isaak heard this answer, he understood that the essence of his journey to Prague was only so that he could hear from the lips of the head of the guards, that it is incumbent upon him to search for treasure, not in a far away place in the king's palace, in Prague, but rather in his own city and in his own room. So Rabbi Isaak traveled home and found the treasure in his room.

The moral of the story is clear: the *hasid* travels to the *tsadik* with the intention of attaining *Yir'at HaShamayim*, but the true *tsadik* will teach him that there is no need to search for the treasure in distant places, i.e. from the *tsadik*. It is possible to find it nearby, in the heart of the *hasid*, "when he will cleanse his heart, his traits and his thoughts he, himself, will find the Divine."

Popular hasidism also differed sharply regarding the role of the *tsadik* in the material affairs of the people. The engagement in the spiritual and physical life of the masses of the people was seen as the main task of popular hasidism. The masses preferred to travel to the Seer of Lublin and to Rabbi Meir Halevi of Apta, both popular *tsadikim*. It was said "...and they judged the people in its time." The Seer of Lublin said, "According to the time and seasons, so they will judge the law." (Exodus 18:22 or 18:26) He interpreted this "judgment in its time," to mean the overseeing of the material situation of the people, to counsel, to heal the sick, to give help and support to the poor and those lacking in a livelihood. He believed that it was incumbent on the *tsadik* to descend from his exalted position to the place of the people. Even if the will of the *tsadik* was to be always in communion with G-d on High, the Seer felt that the will of Hashem, Blessed be He, was for the *tsadik* to be in the practical, material world.

The teaching of Pshis'cha, however, was that the *tsadik* does not have to adapt to the needs of the time and the desires of the people. Rabbi Simcha Bunim believed that the *tsadik* needs to be above his *hasidim*. He explained that, "Each generation has its demands, a generation responds according to the leader and a leader responds according to its generation." This did not mean that the leader should adapt himself to the cultural level of that generation. Leadership within a particular generation meant that if the generation had limited consciousness, the leader needed to have a higher consciousness, so that by his greater spirituality he can influence the limitations of that generation.

For this reason, in Pshis'cha, they diminished the value of the *tsadik*, as the one who is concerned with the material situation of the people. Actually, Rabbi Simcha Bunim was also known for his great love of Israel and, as with all the *tsadikim* of his time, he saw the improvement of the Jewish situation in Poland as a first prerequisite in the elevation of spirituality. Nevertheless, his primary concern was the exaltation of the spiritual condition among his people.

Pshis'cha hasidism and Chabad had a similar approach to this issue. Rabbi Shneur Zalman of Liadi wrote, "Remember the days of old." (Deut. 32.7 Ha'azinu) He questioned what had been done in the past, asking "Was there ever a custom or a regulation to ask for material advice? What should one do about matters of the material world? It is written in Isaiah 3:3 'a counsellor and a skilled artisan', and thus from *Chazal*, we enjoy advice and insight, meaning the words of Torah; which are called insight."

Rabbi Simcha Bunim of Pshis'cha was also

against the dispensing of wonders by *tsadikim*. "Signs and wonders," said Pshis'cha *hasidim*, "are from the descendents of Ham." They saw in them one of the causes for the decline of hasidism and for the development of a limited consciousness, a narrow-mindedness. They believed that the plagues and wonders that were seen in Egypt were signs of the stupidity of the Egyptians.

The aspiration for the revival of the original, true hasidism was one of the fundamentals of Pshis'cha hasidism. The signs of degeneration were already evident. It was caused by the explosive growth of hasidism. Through the influence of the Seer of Lublin and the Magid of Koznits, hasidism had become a popular movement that encompassed all of Judaism, in every part of Poland. However, this growth actually impacted negatively on its inner development. Instead of the profound sweeping vision of hasidism, superficiality and superstition came into every aspect of hasidism. *Tsadikim* became preoccupied in overseeing the material situation, with advice and healings. The first signs of the creation of dynasties, of bequeathing the role of *tsadik* from father to son, also began to appear. *Tsadikim* now appeared, upon whom the crown did not fit at all. In spite of that, they were able to draw to themselves many followers.

The first voice that was raised in the war against the superficiality of popular hasidism was that of the Yehudi HaKadosh (Holy Jew).

Hasidim say that once, Rabbi Simcha Bunim came upon his rabbi, the Yehudi, when he was very sad. The Yehudi said to him,

> *Now and then, the Holy One, Blessed be He, sends to the people of Israel distinguished leaders, former people of spiritual movements who light the path of the Jewish community in the darkness of exile. In the beginning, there were judges, afterwards, prophets, scribes, tannaim, (Mishnaic sages), amoraim, (talmudic sages) each generation and those who seek Him. In the latter time, hasidism appeared as a comforting light to Israel. Now it is also deteriorating. And what will Israel do now?*

Therefore, the Yehudi taught that the *hasidim* should thoroughly examine the *tsadikim*, to see if they are suitable to fulfill their tasks. He once said to Rabbi Simcha Bunim, "Only the person who is connected to the pure hasidism, is pure. Not every person merits the knowledge of connectedness to the really pure hasidism. Many are mistaken and choose false prophets."

Rabbi Simcha Bunim of Pshis'cha waged this war against the degeneration and deterioration of hasidism with even greater vigour. He saw that the masses of the people follow only the externalities. For example, he who wears white silk, a *shtreimel*, and has a pedigree of a good family, is immediately made a *tsadik*. Rabbi Simcha Bunim said that the evil Esau was such a *tsadik*. He also wore clothes of white silk and spoke "torah" at the third meal of Shabbat. For a long time, this warning managed to stop the deterioration of Pshis'cha hasidism.

In Pshis'cha, the *tsadik's* position was not passed on through inheritance for the first few generations. After the departure of Rabbi Simcha Bunim, Rabbi Mendel from Kotsk was chosen; after him, Rabbi Yitschak Meir from Gur, author of *Chidushei Harym*, and after him, Rabbi Chanoch Hacohen from Alexander.

There is a famous story of Rabbi Simcha Bunim's about someone who resembles a deceitful *tsadik*: A peasant, a simple villager, was found rolling around drunk in the street. They took him to a priest's house and washed him and put him into the bed of the priest. They also dressed him in priestly garments worn by the priest, in order to see how the artificial change from a peasant to priest would impact upon him. When the peasant awoke, he saw that he was in the dwelling of a priest, and also in the clothes of a priest, and around him were icons, books, idols and religious texts. The peasant didn't know what had suddenly become of him. If he is a priest, then his memories of being a peasant are only a dream. If he is really a peasant, then what he is seeing with his eyes is only a dream, a night vision. While he was lying on his bed daydreaming, servants entered through his doorway, early in the morning bowing and curtsying opposite him and calling to him, "Greetings our lord, the priest!" The whole matter was a great wonder in his eyes and he couldn't decide if he was a priest or a peasant. Finally, it occurred to him that he should try to read a religious book. If he could understand what was written in it, it would be a sign that he was a priest. If not, then he must be a peasant. He began to study the books and did not understand anything at all! Therefore, he concluded that he was a peasant. But when he got up from his bed, people came to him, honouring him and treating him like a priest. After seeing the belief in his admirers' eyes, he came to the latter conclusion, that actually he is a priest and even though he does not know how to read religious books, it is a sign that the rest of the priests also do not know how to read books.

The moral of the story is: there are so-called 'tsadikim' who receive their status through inheritance from their fathers, and in order to deceive the people, they dress in white clothes. They try to learn through books which they do not understand and the ways of awe and love are far from them. They thereby conclude that their limited knowledge of Torah is not less than that of the remaining tsadikim.

Chapter 17

ISRAEL AND ITS LAND

The love of the people Israel of Polish and Pshis'cha hasidism. The question of Jews. Love of Zion. People of Israel and the nations. Exaltation of the people of Israel. Their eternal holiness. The unity of the people Israel and its land.

The love of Israel occupies a most important place in the teachings and practices of Polish hasidism, as in hasidism in general. They truly endeavoured to carry out the command, "Torah, the Holy One, may He be Blessed, and Israel are one." "Love of Israel," writes one of the Polish *tsadikim*, "is tied to love of the Creator, and it is one, because whoever loves Hashem also loves Israel."

It is impossible to separate out those who commune with G-d, from those who do not also feel the sorrows of the people Israel. All of Israel is one. They are derived from the members of the body of the *Sh'china*, or the holy sparks of the *Sh'china*. And, if G-d forbid, a certain Jew is in distress, then the distress also touches all the way to the One on high, and the holy *Sh'china*, as it were, weeps, "My head is heavy. My arm is heavy. I am totally grief-stricken." (Sanhedrin)

Yet here again, there was a fundamental

143

difference between popular hasidism and that of Pshis'cha. Whereas popular hasidism concerned itself with details of aid, healing, and charity for *hasidim*, Pshis'cha hasidism was destined to belong to an elite circle of scholars. Nevertheless, Rabbi Simcha Bunim recognized the great value inherent in the improvement of their material situation. The love for the people Israel also occupied an important place in the teachings of Rabbi Simcha Bunim.

However, he believed that the essential mission of Israel was '*d'vekut*,' communion with G-d. Therefore, he described the process of material improvement in loftier and more elevated terms. The Pshis'cha *hasidim* aspired to spiritual exaltation, as well as the love of the people Israel and the land of Israel. They accepted a world outlook in which the essence and value of Israel was as a people of G-d, and the land of Israel was seen as their rightful holy place.

Rabbi Simcha Bunim, was a sophisticated, modern man who was familiar with the political and cultural life of European peoples. He understood full well their deteriorating economic situation and that it was impossible to solve the 'Jewish question' merely through charity and acts of kindness. He knew that fundamental change required a much larger effort. Rabbi Bunim, as reported by the *maskil*, Yitschak of Yasz, said to a high government official that the government had an obligation to improve the material conditions of Polish Jewry, as well as to reduce the numbers of poor people.

According to the testimony of Rabbi Yisrael of Kotsk, the grandson of Rabbi Mendel of Kotsk, and a member of *Chovevei Tsion*, (Lovers of Zion), Rabbi Simcha Bunim was amazed when he heard about Rabbi Moshe Montifiore's political activities, which were directed toward the material welfare of Jews in the land of Israel and the diasporas. When *hasidim* asked Rabbi Bunim, "What is the point in acquiring the soil of the land of Israel when we still have not experienced the coming of the Messiah?" he replied, "If the soil of the land of Israel will be redeemed from the hands of the Arabs and will be given to the Jews, the redemption will come immediately."

The breadth and depth of Pshis'cha's hasidism was in sharp contrast to that of popular hasidism, which concentrated primarily on *Kabalah* and the *Zohar*. Pshis'cha *hasidim* diligently studied the literature of medieval philosophy. When Rabbi Simcha Bunim spoke about the special virtue of the Jewish people, and their communion with G-d and the land of Israel, the influence of the *Kuzari* of Rabbi Yehudah Halevi was evident. The influence of the Maharal of Prague was especially apparent, as witnessed by his book, *Netsach Yisrael, (The Eternal Israel)* in which the Maharal clarified the essence of Israel, its communion with G-d and its mission, in such a way that it appeared very close to the outlook of Rabbi Simcha Bunim.

According to the teachings of Pshis'cha, the people of Israel are the beloved of G-d. Israel was called a "people close to Him' because they are close to the Holy One, may He be Blessed. Just as relatives are tied to one another, so they are tied to Him from deep within their souls. It is their very nature: they follow after Him, whether willingly or unwillingly. It is impossible to totally explain the essence of this attraction or make it intelligible. Even from the less educated people to the most ignorant among the people of Israel and those who have no knowledge at all, they would all sacrifice themselves for "*Kiddush Hashem,*" the holiness of G-d. Such is the nature of their very souls and the love that is within them. So deeply are they tied to the Holy One.

This assigned special love is hidden. Although there is one creator for all things and creatures, and He alone forms everything, the consciousness of a certain moral standard of the Jewish people surpasses that of the rest of the nations. The essential intention of the creation was for the sake of Israel, and the Jewish people are seen as the crown of the creatures and nations of the world. Israel resembles a son who tries to please his Father who is in heaven, and the Holy One, may He be Blessed, receives delight and joy from him.

The Holy One, Blessed be He, apportioned a part of His wisdom and His majesty to Israel, his only son, and granted it upon him. The

Creator, may He be Blessed, created the world in order to do good for His creatures and to bestow upon them His goodness. He sustains them and provides for all their needs. His great kindness endures forever. He bequeathed to His people, Israel, the ultimate goodness, i.e. the seed of our holy forefathers. He did this so that they could recognize His greatness and His splendour and the extent of His goodness. His final success can be seen in that there is no other G-d before Him.

This love between the Holy One, Blessed be He, and Israel, also imposes many obligations on the Jewish people. This acknowledgement of the Divine is conditional on a life of holiness and the exaltation of the spirit, along with the merit and loving kindness that Israel received from G-d, were also obligations and exalted tasks.

In order to achieve this ultimate goodness, G-d forbade us from all the evil lusts by warning us of the punishments which would occur if we were to trespass His *mitsvot*. Israel does not necessarily do the *mitsvot* willingly and voluntarily, but rather, it is more like paying a debt, because the Holy One, Blessed be He, planted within them His portion. As it is said, "…because a part of G-d is with them" (Deut. 32:9) and "From all the families of the earth, I knew only you, therefore I remembered you."(Amos 3:2) With that same knowing of G-d and a life of holiness, it is, therefore, incumbent on Israel to be a model and a guide to all the other creatures. Rabbi Simcha Bunim quotes the

Maharal saying, "Israel is in the role of a male who desires to bestow, and the other nations are in the role of the female who do not desire to give but rather to receive."

Everything that is said about Avraham, our father, is also said about his children. Avraham wished to make G-d's divinity known to all those in his world and that was his sole purpose in life, i.e. that all the creatures would recognize who gave them life, would esteem Him and would praise G-d's greatness. This is the primary task of Israel in its exile among the nations of the world. They will be a light unto the nations. This vision will keep Israel from assimilating among the nations. Even when they may be exiled in impure places, they will keep their holiness and their virtue, which is essentially their *d'vekut*, communion with the Divine. "You are exalted above all tongues." (Liturgy, Festival Musaf Amidah) Rabbi Simcha Bunim explained this prayer in this way: The love that is between the Holy One, Blessed be He, and Israel is so pure and lofty that no language in the world has the power to explain it. The language of humans is poor and speech is too clumsy to express the very essence of this noble love. The exaltation of loving kindness is above all languages. Israel is pure and holy in its very essence. They are the children of G-d and cleave to Him with all their strength in true inner communion.

In Israel, it is impossible that sin, itself,

will be inherent in the person, but rather it can only come about through happenstance. Rabbi Simcha Bunim said that, "the sins of Israel are transient but the holiness of Israel is eternal." The image of our ancient Israelite ancestors is engraved in the souls of the transgressors so that their very essence is pure and not flawed by sins. Therefore, communion with G-d dwells within them. Holiness after a time can grow within them and their sins will cease. As the Pshis'cha teachings would say, "The ways of G-d are straight."

In *midrash*, it appears that Yitschak looked upon the transgressors of Israel in a spiritual way so that they too would sanctify Hashem. When the holiness is hidden, one may not know how much development is needed for that holiness to go forth to the light. Holiness generally emerges by connecting with the sinners because you cannot extract the dross, the base metal, from the silver except through a smelting process, which is a complete unification of the silver with the dross. Thus the silver is purified and becomes separated. It is similar to the time when Yaacov and Esav were being formed in one womb. Like the smelting of the silver and the base metal, from that process a part of holiness emerged. Therefore, it is proper to see in every Jew only his higher qualities and not focus on his deficiencies. "Please go and see to the well-being of your brother," Yaacov says to Yosef. (Genesis 37:14) In other words, see the wholeness of your brothers and not just their deficiencies. This trait is a branch of humility, to see only the good in others. According to the teaching of Pshis'cha, it is one of the fundamentals of Judaism and he who does not believe in this is a heretic.

The Jewish people have maintained a profound connectedness to the land of Israel. Other nations do not have this kind of spiritual relationship with a special place. The people of Israel have exalted the land of Israel and yearn for the inheritance of their land. By elevating their minds in exaltation, the people Israel and the land are one. They feel that they can totally develop their true selves, only in the land of Israel.

Rabbi Simcha Bunim taught that only in the land of Israel will their complete essence be revealed. Outside the land of Israel, one cannot be capable of worship as one can in the land of Israel. The pure love that is between the Jewish people and the holy land is very powerful. This love is analogous to the love and marriage between a bride and groom who dwell together, not because of some external reason like money, beauty, family or other reasons, but rather, because "the bride and groom love each other without any connection to an external benefit." Rabbi Simcha Bunim said that their fundamental desire is to cleave together in love without a third person between them. This is called *yichud*, a complete union. Likewise, the people Israel and the land are destined for each other and therefore, one can say, "how good and pleasant is their dwelling together." (Psalms 133:1)

This marriage, that is the total union of the people Israel and their land, will reach its complete fulfillment at the time of the redemption, when the Messiah will come. According to the teaching of Pshis'cha, the coming of the hoped-for Messiah will happen in a simple way. If his soul will be fit enough to let the light of redemption appear upon it, then every Jew has the potential to be the Messiah. According to Rabbi Simcha Bunim,

> In general, the capacity to be the Messiah resides in all of the people of Israel and when G-d will want to redeem His people, He will choose the one with that potential. He will appear above Him who is on High, and will reveal to him the light of the Messiah and thus he will be the redeemer, may He speedily be revealed.

In the future, when a complete redemption of Israel will occur, the holiness of the Hebrew language will also be revealed, our holy tongue. In our time, it exists today as translation. In the future, it will be recognized as the holy tongue. Then there will be a perfect union: a unity among the people Israel, the union of a people, their land and their tongue, and communion of Israel with its G-d.

Chapter 18

PARABLES AND SAYINGS

What you get for nothing—is not really valued. Eyes of the heart. An exemplary guard. The sin of the lamb. The end of one who imitates. Daring ascenders. My innermost self weeps. (Jeremiah 13:17) I am a prayer. (Psalm 109:4) A perverse and crooked generation. (Deut.32:5) They both acknowledged a covenant. (Gen. 21:27) A mitsvah that is not for its own sake.

When asked, "Why don't you write a book," Rabbi Simcha Bunim of Pshis'cha replied, "I wanted to write a book and call it 'The Generations of Adam" because it would contain all the generations of man, his essence and his tasks." Although never written, Rabbi Simcha Bunim was truly a master in the "generations of man". While his parables generally illustrate his understanding and awareness of the secrets of mankind, in particular, they highlight his extraordinary intelligence. All the great ones of that generation, especially the Seer of Lublin, called him *hachacham* Rabbi Bunim, "the sage". Since a sage is preferable to a prophet, this is where the power of his influence lay.

Like Rabbi Nachman of Bratslav, Rabbi

Simcha Bunim loved to tell parables and other stories, which he told with literary artistry and intelligence. His very pointed parables aimed at explaining lofty ideas concerning man and how the influence of the world is great upon their souls, as shown in the following examples of his parables and sayings.

What You Get For Nothing — Is Not Really Valued

Businessmen and *mitnagdim* came to Rabbi Simcha Bunim and asked him, "Why are our sons-in-law, young men, distinguished students of Torah, leaving their families and sitting for successive weeks in Pshis'cha in order to learn about the *yir'ah* of G-d? Isn't the learning at home of *Reshit Chochma, (Beginning of Wisdom),* and *Shevet Musar, (The Tribe of Musar),* sufficient? Why is traveling so far from home and with so many expenses necessary?" Rabbi Simcha Bunim answered them with a parable:

Two doctors live in the same city. One of them is good-hearted and satisfied with a small payment and he is well accepted by the inhabitants of the city. The second physician is expensive and prescribes expensive medicines, and many people in the city come early to the entrance of his office.

The reason for this is clear. As soon as someone gets sick, they immediately visit the less expensive doctor who treats them at a modest cost and writes out a prescription for the

153

pharmacist. But, as is often the case with sick people, many of them are not in a hurry to fill the expensive prescription. In the meantime, the sickness worsens and they call on the doctor again. Thinking that the patient had taken the previous medication and that it did not benefit him, the doctor writes another prescription, which really is not necessary. Now the condition of the sick person becomes much more serious.

With the expensive doctor, however, the situation is entirely different. They only call him in the event of a mortal illness and at that point, they are no longer concerned about the cost. They comply with all his instructions and so the people are healed.

Eyes of The Heart

Some people wondered aloud to Rabbi Simcha Bunim why he did not try to cure his blindness. He replied, "That which is good for me to see, I see with the eyes of my heart. That which is not fitting to see, why should I see it at all!"

An Exemplary Guard

A high ranking official had a noble horse that was very dear to him. He watched over her, like the apple of his eye. The gate of the stable was closed and locked and he had a special watchman who sat day and night beside her. One night the official became anxious and couldn't sleep. He went to the stable to see how the horse was faring. The watchman sat and watched but it was obvious that he was sunk deep in thought. "What are you reflecting on?" asked the official. "I am perplexed," he replied. "When one hammers a nail into the wall, where does the wood from the hole disappear to?" "Correct thoughts," said the official and he returned to his house and lay down to sleep. But he couldn't sleep. Anxiety filled his soul. Once again he went to the stable and found the watchman sunk in thought. "What are you thinking?" asked the official. "I'm perplexed," answered the watchman. "When a man eats a bagel, where does the hole in the middle disappear to?" "Good thoughts," said the official and he returned home, but still he could not fall asleep. So he returned for a third time to see if the horse was still being well and truly guarded. "What are you engaged in now?" asked the official. "I am perplexed," replied the watchman. "The gate is closed and the bolts are securely fastened. I am closely and carefully guarding and the horse is gone! What is the reason for this?"

The Sin of The Lamb

A poor man from a good family once came to the city of Bandin, in Poland. He was barefoot and hungry. A young *hasid* saw his misfortune and took pity on the visitor. The *hasid* emptied the synagogue's charity box that was designated for the purchase of books, with the intention of eventually returning the money. He gave the poor man food to eat and clothes to wear. When the matter became known to the caretakers of the synagogue, they called a general meeting of the congregation to judge the *hasid*, the thief. Rabbi Simcha Bunim related a parable relevant to this occurrence:

Once a plague erupted among the animals and beasts, and many deaths befell them. They turned to the king of beasts, the lion, to find out what was to be done to stop the plague. The lion called a general meeting and all the animals gave their opinions and advice, which did not please the king. The clever fox in the group spoke last, offering his smart suggestion. "My lord king! My opinion is that there is no punishment without sin. Certainly we have sinned. We have transgressed and therefore this plague is upon us. We must remove the evil that is in our midst and stop the plague." They responded unanimously, "Beautiful explanation. Beautifully spoken," they cried. They immediately set up a court of experts to sit and judge the sinners and transgressors, declaring in a loud voice, "Let everyone who has sinned come forth and confess his sin."

The tiger came first and confessed his sin, the sin of murder. Courageous hunters were pursuing him and he almost fell into their hands. However, a miracle happened and he escaped from them. He was tired and very hungry and when he saw a man innocently walking by, the tiger attacked and devoured him. The judges and experts heard his testimony. They considered the matter and exonerated the tiger, saying that he devoured the person in order to nourish himself. They said that he did this because he was hungry and not because his heart was evil, G-d forbid! Besides the fact that the hunters had pursued him, he was gripped with an intense hunger and it felt like there was almost nothing between him and death. He is not guilty because the principle "to save a life" overrides murder.

A wolf came forth and proclaimed his sin. "Once, I went out to hunt prey in order to fill my hungry stomach. I saw a cow with her calf alongside her in the meadow. My hunger gripped me so tightly that I felt as if I would pass out. I devoured the cow and her off-spring at once. I have sinned. I have done an iniquity. I have transgressed." The judges studied the case of the wolf and found that he did not warrant punishment because the way of the wolf is naturally to hunt prey. A wolf lives by means of hunting and what would happen to a wolf if he did not hunt prey?

Finally, an innocent lamb came forth. She bowed before the king and cried bitterly, "I have surely sinned. All this suffering is because of me. There was a harsh and bitter winter this year and I nearly froze to death. My owner was kind and took pity on me and put me in his room. The man put straw into his boots in order to keep his feet warm and every night I ate the straw because I was hungry. But the owner did not know it. My sin is so hard to bear." All the animals and beasts unanimously cheered and shouted, "You have indeed sinned and there is no other sinner like you. You are the reason for our misfortune. The owner showed you kindness and mercy and you repaid him with evil for his goodness. Death to the sinner!" They immediately decreed a judgment of a horrible death and tore her to pieces.

The End of One Who Imitates

A man passing by the palace of the king saw the king gesturing to one of his officials, who was approaching, and the official discussed something with him. The official immediately went out, gave an order to an army battalion, and brought the battalion to the king. At another time, the same man returned to the front of the palace and once again he saw the king gesture. It seemed to the man as though the nod was for him. He promptly went to the king, expecting to also converse with the king, thinking that the king would soon appoint him to head a battalion. But, to his chagrin, policemen came and expelled him from the palace. Thus the man concluded that there are gestures, and there are gestures. It all depends on how and to whom one is gesturing. One should not merely look at situations superficially and then imitate. The context around each situation is different.

Daring Ascenders

A king lived in a magnificently built palace, with room after room and floor upon floor. In order to reach the room of the king, one had to pass through many complicated staircases and no one had, as yet, succeeded in seeing the king. Many people had tried to enter and find their way. But, ultimately they returned the way they had come. There were those who turned back in the middle of the way, and there were those who ascended most of the staircases, but still had been unable to reach the king. However, a clever person came along and decided to make signs along the staircases. Little by little each day, he would advance and ascend, descend and ascend, according to the signs he had made. Finally he was able to reach the king.

My Innermost Self Weeps (Jeremiah 13:17)

A son of a king sinned and his father banished him. He was exiled and sent wandering from city to city, and country to country. The father took pity on his son and hid for him, a treasure of jewels and costly pearls in the king's palace. He intended to give him this treasure when he would repent and return home. It happened that a fire broke out in the palace of the king and burned everything. The son still had not turned away from his evil ways. The court officials wept for the burning of the palace, but the king cried with heartrending sobs for the

159

unrepentant son, who had not returned to claim the hidden treasure which awaited him.

I Am a Prayer (Psalm 109:4)

When a needy person is dressed in pleasant clothes, he needs to justify his neediness and ask people to have mercy on him. But when he is dressed in tatters and cast off clothes, there is no need for pleading and words. His neediness is obvious by his clothes. His lowly and depressed appearance demands compassion. His appearance pleads his case. As they say, "I am (by my mere appearance) a prayer."

A Perverse and Crooked Generation (Deut.32:5)

"Once, I was sitting in a Jewish restaurant in Danzig, on a Friday night," Rabbi Simcha Bunim said. "A Jew entered and asked for a drink of wine. There were two waiters, a Jew and a Christian. They both went down to the cellar to bring up the wine. The Jew lit a candle, in order to provide light for the Christian to bring up the wine for the Jew."

They Both Acknowledged a Covenant (Gen. 21:27)

Rabbi Simcha Bunim once told his *hasidim* to enter a pub in Warsaw. They sat and paid attention to a conversation between two Jewish porters who were drinking. One asked, "Did you learn the Torah section already?" "Yes," answered the other one, "but I had difficulty with one thing. It is written about Avraham and Avimelech that 'both of them made a covenant.' Why did it say 'both of them'?" The first porter replied to him, "I would think that the explanation is like this. Although Avraham and Avimelech acknowledged a covenant together, they did not turn into one person. They still remained two distinct individuals."

A *Mitsvah* That Is Not For Its Own Sake

Everyone who does a *mitsvah* that is not for its own sake, but rather is mixed with one's selfishness, is like he who worships idols. There is no difference between worshiping idols and worshiping one's self.

GLOSSARY

Ahavah – literally means "love". The spiritual state associated with the *sefirah* of *chesed*.

Anavah – literally means "humility" or "unpretentiousness", a nullification of the ego, a paramount ideal within Judaism. Moses is referred to as "exceedingly humble, more than any man in the world." (Bamidbar 12:3)

Asiyah – denotes the physical world, the world of action. *Asiyah* is the lowest of the four worlds of creation.

Atsilut – the first and highest of the four worlds of creation and represents a closeness to the Divine.

Binah – literally means "understanding". *Binah* is the third of the ten *sefirot*, and the second conscious power of intellect in Creation.

Birkat HaMazon – set of blessings that were formulated to be recited after a meal.

Briyah – denotes the world of creation and intellect and is the second highest of the four worlds.

Bitul (Bitul Hayesh) – means self-nullification, selflessness, or annihilation. Any number of states of selflessness or self-abnegation. The spiritual state associated with the inner experience of *chochmah*.

162

Chazal – an acronym, *"chet"*, *"zayin"*, *"lamed"*. The *"chet"* stands for *Chachameinu*, "Our Sages" and the *"zayin"* and *"lamed"* correspond to the expression *"Zichronam l'vracho"* meaning "Of Blessed Memory". It is used to designate the authoritative opinion of the Talmud.

Cheder (pl. chadarim) – literally means a "room". Traditionally, it referred to an elementary level Jewish school.

Chochmah – literally means "wisdom". *Chochmah* is the second of the ten *sefirot*, and the first power of conscious intellect within creation.

Chozeh – a seer.

Da'at – literally means "knowledge". The third and last conscious power of intellect in creation, counted as one of the ten *sefirot* when *keter*, the superconscious, is not counted. It is the unifying force within the ten *sefirot*.

Devekut – literally means a "clinging" or a "cleaving" to G-d, which was the aspiration of the righteous person.

Emunah – literally means "faith". The belief that no matter what G-d does, it is all ultimately for the greatest good, even if it does not appear so to us at the present time. The spiritual state associated with an

163

inner experience.

Gaon (pl. Geonim) – two meanings, one "historical", the other in common usage, both based from the root meaning "pride". The "historical" meaning refers to the Group of Torah Scholars who followed the *"Amoraim"*. The more common meaning is "Torah genius". Often it is a title of respect for a great scholar. It is one of the highest forms of praise to be considered a *"gaon"*.

Gemara – in Aramaic, literally means "to study". The part of the Talmud that contains rabbinical commentaries and analysis of the core component, the *Mishnah*.

Halacha – from the Hebrew word meaning "to walk". This is the legal part of rabbinical literature that legislates the practical application of the Torah for everyday life. Thus *"halacha"* can be defined as rulings or teachings on "how to walk with G-d".

Hasid (pl. hasidim) – followers of hasidism.

Hasidut, hasidism – a Jewish mystical revival movement founded by Israel Ba'al Shem Tov that arose in early 18th century in Ukraine, teaching closeness to G-d through simple piety, ecstatic prayer and also the notion of bringing *Kabalah* to everyone in some form.

Haskalah – literally means "enlightenment". An intellectual movement in Europe that lasted from approximately the 1770s to the 1880s and represented Judaism as a non-dogmatic, rational faith that is open to modernity and change.

Kabalah – Jewish mysticism. The basic book is the *"Zohar"* pseudo-epigraphically attributed to Rabbi Shimon bar Yochai. (see *Zohar*).

Kavanah (pl. "Kavanot") – conscious thought, intention, concentration.

Maariv – the daily evening prayer.

Magid – an itinerant storyteller-preacher, usually among the early hasidic community.

Maskil (pl. maskilim) – a follower of *haskalah*.

Midah (pl. Midot) – literally means "characteristic", "measure" or "attribute", Divine or human. One of the thirteen attributes of mercy, which are part of the revelation of the *sefirah keter* and may represent any of the *sefirot* from *chesed* to *malchut*, in contrast to the higher *sefirot* of the intellect.

Midrash (pl. Midrashim) – literally meaning "something that is derived". The *Midrash* is the second major body of the oral Torah (after the Talmud), consisting of halachic or homiletic material couched as linguistic analyses of the Biblical text.

Minchah – the daily afternoon prayer.

Mitnaged (pl. mitnagdim) – literally means "opponents". This term was used to refer to Ashkenazi religious Jews who opposed *hasidim*.

Mitsvah (pl. mitsvot) – literally means "commandment". Idiomatically referred to as a good deed. One of the six hundred and thirteen commandments given by G-d to the Jewish people at Mt. Sinai, or seven commandments given by G-d to the nations of the world.

Mussar – morality, ethics; reproof or punishment. A moral movement, based on the study of traditional ethical literature.

Posek (pl. poskim) – literally meaning "arbiter". A rabbinical scholar and authority who decides in disputes and halachic questions.

Rebbe – literally meaning "my teacher". It referred originally to hasidic masters. The term denoted the relationship between the master and his followers. The term is also used to describe or address a teacher of Torah.

Sefirah (pl. Sefirot) – A *sefirah* is a channel of Divine energy or life-force. It is via the *sefirot* that G-d interacts with creation; thus they may be considered G-d's "attributes".

Shacharit – the daily morning prayer.

Shechinah – the Divine "indwelling" Presence. The *Shechinah* is the immanent Divine Presence that dwells within the universe, corresponding to the *sefirah* of *malchut*, the "feminine" aspect of Divinity.

Shema – the *"Shema Yisrael"*, "Hear O' Israel" prayer, named after its opening words, is a compilation of three Biblical passages (Deuteronomy 6:4-9, 11:13-21, Numbers 15:37-41) which Jews are commanded to recite twice daily. The first verse is the fundamental profession of monotheism, "Hear O' Israel, G-d is our G-d, G-d is one."

Shofar (pl. shofarot) – a ram's horn; blown on various significant occasions.

Shtetl – a small town in Eastern Europe, partly or predominantly Jewish prior to 1939.

Shulchan Aruch – literally means a "Set Table". An important repository of Jewish Law, compiled originally by Rabbi Yosef Karo.

Siddur (pl. siddurim) – from the Hebrew word for "order" because it establishes the proper order for the recitation of prayers. It is the Jewish Prayer Book used on

Shabbat and weekdays throughout the year.

Talmud – repository of "Oral Law" of Judaism; consists of *Mishnah* and *Gemara*.

Tefilah (pl. "Tefilot") – literally means "prayer" The *Tefilah* often refers to the standing meditative prayer known as the "*Amidah*".

T'vunah – literally means "comprehension". It is developed from the *sefirah* of *binah*.

Tosafot – writings of a group of Rashi Torah Scholars, mainly his grandsons and great grandsons.

Tsadik (pl. "Tsadikim") – a righteous man, based on the Hebrew word "*tsedek*", or "justice". The "*tsadik*" is one who conquers his "evil inclinations", towards pride, power, and oppression, and practices righteousness and humility. In hasidism, the *tsadik* denotes a special type of spiritual leader.

Tsedakah – comes from the root "*tsedek*", meaning "justice" or "righteousness". In general society, it is associated with the word "charity", helping one who is less fortunate than oneself.

Tshuvah – literally means "returning". Commonly referred to as "repentance". After a period of estrangement, the individual returns to a state of oneness with, and commitment to, G-d and His

Torah.

Tsimtsum – literally means "contraction". It connotes the concept of contraction and "removal" of G-d's infinite light in order to allow for creation of independent realities.

Yeshivah (pl. "Yeshivot") – Torah academy.

Yetsirah – the world of emotion and formation. *Yetsirah* is the third of the four worlds of creation.

Yir'ah – literally means a combination of "fear", "awe" and "reverence". "*Yir'at Hashem*" or "*Yir'at Shamayim*" is the sense of awe of G-d's presence.

Zohar – literally means "splendour". The *Zohar* is the seminal work of the *Kabalah*, pseudo epigraphically attributed to Rabbi Shimon bar Yochai, a second century *Tanna*. It is a collection of works by Moses de Leon, who lived in Spain during the 12th century and considered the classic mystical commentary on sections of the Torah.

ISBN 1425128900-4